A HISTORICAL
SURVEY OF
ANTI-SEMITISM

A HISTORICAL SURVEY OF ANTI-SEMITISM

Richard E. Gade

BAKER BOOK HOUSE
Grand Rapids, Michigan 49506

PHOTOLITHOPRINTED BY CUSHING - MALLOY, INC.
ANN ARBOR, MICHIGAN, UNITED STATES OF AMERICA

Contents

CHAPTER 1

Origins

The term *anti-Semitism* was coined by a German agitator, Wilhelm Marr,[1] in 1879 to designate anti-Jewish campaigns then appearing throughout Europe. Since that time the term has been universally applied to any form of behavior, activity, or literature which evidences hostility toward the Jews. In this survey, we will begin by looking at the earliest occurrences of anti-Semitic feeling in the ancient world. We will follow the paths of Jewry along the long roads of Diaspora, looking at the Jewish community in the early Christian period as well as in its first contacts with Islam. We will examine the Jewry of the Middle Ages, the Reformation, the Renaissance, and the Age of Enlightenment; we will trace its progress through the dawn of our "modern" times into the holocaust of the Second World War. Finally, we will observe the state of Jewry as it reemerges into the light of political history with the formation of the Jewish State and moves rapidly to the forefront of world affairs.

The story is not a pleasant one, and the parties involved may sometimes come as a surprise. It is not our intention to condemn or applaud, but simply to state what history remembers of the lot of the chosen people as they moved through the ages of Western civilization.

During the Old Testament period, Israel had her enemies as well as her allies; but it appears that she was not troubled by what we would now term anti-Semitic prejudices. Her situation was that of a small kingdom occupying a region critical to the socio-political strategies of her powerful neighbors—Egypt, Babylon, Assyria, Persia, Greece, and Rome. They all had their day before the gates of the Holy City, and each conquest wove its own influences into the fabric of Jewish culture. Yet the Jew retained his strong sense of identity, his divine sanction, throughout years of captivity and exile. Through the labors of her prophets and teachers, Israel divorced herself from the fluctuations of history, clinging to her ancient laws and struggling to resist acculturation that would have submerged her forever in the currents of Western society.

The first major occurrence of blatant anti-Semitic sentiment, therefore, fell within the arena of the Greco-Roman world. Alexander's generals, having divided the empire at the time of Alexander's death, established dynasties of their own, stretching from the Indus Valley to the Straits of Gibraltar and from Egypt to the south of Europe. This period saw the flowering of Hellenistic culture throughout the Mediterranean region, and the Greek rulers looked upon themselves as champions of the superior ideals of Greek civilization. The resistant Jew, as they saw him, stood in the path of the fulfillment of this cultural mission.[2] The Ptolemies ruled in Egypt; the Seleucids in Syria. In matters of conflict, the Jews traditionally sided with the more tolerant and restrained Ptolemies. The Seleucids, on the other hand, campaigned avidly to stamp out all resistance to Greek modes of thinking. During the reign of Antiochus IV Epiphanes[3] (175–

163 B.C.), repeated harassment poured out of Syria in efforts to crush the arrogant Jew. The coup d'etat was delivered by Antiochus himself, who, after subjugating Jerusalem, moved into the temple precincts and sacrificed a swine on the altar. To complete his desecration of Judaism's most sacred site, he ordered the blood from the sacrificial animal sprinkled on the volumes of law containing statutes pertaining to the Gentile world.[4] Antiochus returned northward, leaving an outraged Jewish populace.

During the reign of John Hyrcanus,[5] the Syrians again besieged Jerusalem. After a year's resistance, Hyrcanus was obliged to surrender. At this time the Syrian generals counseled their king to annihilate the inhabitants of the city, pointing out that the Jews were the only people in the world who refused to associate with their neighbors in social and religious matters. To the Greek, this introverted arrogance was seen as misanthropy, thwarting the progress of Hellenistic unification. Antiochus stopped short of genocide, however, and returned to his rapidly deteriorating domestic affairs.[6]

Hyrcanus's successors (the Hasmonaean rulers) extended control over much of Palestine and retaliated against those centers of Gentile population which had sided with the Syrian invaders. Political and religious oppression was the order of the day. Coinciding with these popular vendettas there appeared the first of many centuries of anti-Semitic legends. Egyptian legends[7] about oppressive shepherd-kings and a leprous subject people who had been expelled in order to purify a defiled Egypt were linked to the story of the Exodus in order to point out that the "uncleanliness" and separateness of the Jew were the result of his origins, and that these origins were directly responsible for his present habits. The Syrian rulers regarded the Jew as a nomad, a status that justified his eradication in pursuit of the Greek goal of a perfected humanity. As the Hasmonaeans sought to purge idolatry from Israel to preserve the sanctity of their religious inheritance, it is not difficult to imagine the reaction of Israel's pagan neighbors. The Jewish presence in the land was viewed as both a threat and an injustice.

As Roman rule spread throughout the eastern Mediterranean, open conflict between Jews and Gentiles subsided. Political revolt and intrigue were not regarded as great threats by Rome. For a time, large portions of the Jewish populace wholeheartedly adopted Gentile ways. Fuel for anti-Semitism came from another source—the growth of the imperial cults inaugurated by Augustus. Here the line was drawn in terms of social accommodation. Since the emperor ruled by divine authority, emperor worship was, to the Roman, an act of loyalty to the state, imbued with a sense of religious sanctity. Refusal to participate, therefore, constituted refusal to accept the authority of the state. The feeling spread that since the Jews alone balked at such obeisance, they therefore had no respect for humanity or those things that humanity held in esteem. The emperor Caligula[8] ordered his image erected in Jerusalem in an attempt to quash Jewish resistance, and it appears he was prepared to force the issue; however, his assassination postponed the conflict with imperial emissaries and doubtlessly saved much turmoil.

The Jews of the Roman period, however, did not face the outright segregation of later centuries. Jews were found throughout the empire, concentrated in urban areas (their total population has been estimated at from six to ten million[9]), where they enjoyed the social flexibility of any other citizen in regard to occupation and legal position. In some cases they were even afforded special privileges in deference to their religious observances. These exclusive privileges[10] sometimes extended into areas of civic responsibility borne by the rest of the populace. Persian, Greek, and early Roman rulers judiciously guarded Jewish interests; and save for dramatic exceptions, i.e. Antiochus Epiphanes, from the Persian period to the first century B.C. Judaism was left to itself, at least officially. As had been the case in Babylonian exile, many Jews acquired great wealth and power, even occupying high government positions.

During the first century B.C. the status of the Jew steadily declined. In Alexandria, the former Ptolemaic aristocracy (put out of power by Roman rule) found itself on a social level equal to that of the Jews, with whom they now competed for Roman favor. Riots directed against the Jews erupted at the instigation of Greek residents of the city. The situation spread to other cities in the empire until it became necessary for the emperor Claudius to intervene. In his edict, Claudius reaffirmed the rights of his Jewish subjects but hastened to enjoin them to more hospitable behavior concerning their fellows. He warned that if his wishes were not observed, he would take whatever actions he deemed necessary to deal with these people who had spread "a general plague throughout the world."[11] It seems the Jew had come to be regarded as a distinct threat by powerful segments of the Roman population.

Roman law remained unchanged, but anti-Semitism spread into literary and intellectual circles, where the Jews came to be regarded as disrespectful of the law and the mainstream of humanity as a whole. The ancient legends concerning Jewish uncleanliness again gained prominence, and malicious rumors (i.e. tales of human sacrifice in the Jerusalem temple) were fostered by men such as Chaeremon (Nero's tutor),[12] Lysimachus (librarian of Alexandria),[13] and Apion (a widely-read poet-philosopher).[14] A period of eschatological fervor overtook Roman religious thinking and various redemptive teachings appeared at this time (i.e. the Eleusinian Mysteries, Cult of Isis, etc.). For a brief interlude, the message of Judaism seemed to be rising in favor, but with the destruction of the second temple the anti-Jewish "intellectuals" seized the opportunity to point to the act as a sign of God's hatred of this people.[15] The situation deteriorated rapidly with anti-Semitic uprisings occurring throughout the empire.

Increased foreign influences in Rome itself contributed to a general distrust of the Jews by the aristocracy, who sought a return to a purer, earlier form of rule, free of outside influences. The emperors methodically snuffed out the last vestiges of freedom in Roman life. A dictatorship in the modern sense overtook Roman politics, and the city smoldered in an atmosphere of distrust and corruption. Any foreign influence came to be regarded as subversive to the high ideals of Roman life. With widespread popular success, writers such as Horace,[16] Martial,[17] and Cicero[18] hurled literary barbs at the Jewish population.

By the end of the first century A.D., the Jews were under full-fledged attack by upper-class writers who sought to rally support to their cause by making a life-and-death battle out of the struggle against Judaic influences, which were especially widespread in the middle and lower classes. The highly respected writer Tacitus[19] cited the Greek anti-Semitic literature of earlier centuries in his *Historiae*, in which he claims to have inquired into the validity of the Greek charges and found them borne out by historical fact. His vehement attacks had a great impact on public sentiment, as did those of Juvenal,[20] whose poetry proved highly derisive to the status and social image of the Jews. All these efforts had, luckily for the Jews, little influence on the Roman lawmakers (except for the brief period of anti-Jewish policy under Hadrian);[21] but the lot of the Jewish community had been dealt a death blow. The precedent had been set for the centuries to follow.

CHAPTER 2

The Early Christian Period

The year 70 A.D. marked a crisis in Jewish history, for in that year the Roman general Titus besieged and sacked Jerusalem, burning the temple and bringing an abrupt end to the political life of the Hebrew state. So began a new era of Jewish history, one which saw the widespread dispersion of the Jewish people. The arena of Judaic life spread far outside the national boundaries of the former state, from Spain to India, across North Africa, and north into Britain and other parts of Europe. Sages and mystics, scholars and martyrs, occupy the pages of the story which once knew prophets and kings. As the state vanished, however, the zealous preservation of ancient laws and holy orders went on.

Even as the walls of Jerusalem were crumbling, the wheels of change were moving. Abandoning the doomed city, a small group of men led by one Johanan ben Zakkai rallied what remained of Israel's scholars and teachers and quickly established a school of Torah in the city of Jabneh. With temple worship now impossible, these *tanna*, or teachers, turned to the prophet Hosea for the apologetics of their school: "I desire mercy and not sacrifice, and the knowledge of God rather than burnt offerings."[1] This school marked the beginning of the long centuries of adjustment and intellectual flowering that were to lead to the collection of works known as the *Mishnah*.

The synagogue began to fill the place of authority once occupied by the temple, and prayers and the study of the Torah were offered in place of sacrifices. On the surface, things seemed to be moving in a positive direction, but the bitterness of conquest lingered in the memory of a proud people. Roman taxes supposedly exacted for the reconstruction of the temple were instead poured into the construction of the temple of Jupiter in Rome.[2] This deceit, coupled with a drive for empire on the part of the emperor Trajan (which brought the flourishing Jewish community in Mesopotamia under Roman rule), fanned revolt; and in the year 115 A.D.[3] the Jews rose in savage fury to challenge Rome's might. Contemporary chroniclers[4] record casualties in the hundreds of thousands. The revolt seems to have been led by two brothers, Pappus and Julianus,[5] but it was quickly crushed by Lucius Quietus,[6] the Roman governor of Judah.

Trajan's successor, Aelius Hadrian, abandoned the provinces of Mesopotamia and seemingly adopted a policy of conciliation, even promising to rebuild the Jerusalem temple. He recalled Quietus to Rome and ordered him executed.[7] The promise of a temple was not kept; instead, in 130 A.D. Hadrian ordered Jerusalem rebuilt as a Roman city, Aelia Capitolina,[8] with a temple to Jupiter occupying the temple site. In a later edict,[9] Hadrian revived an ancient Roman law forbidding mutilation, thus outlawing the rite of circumcision as practiced by the Jews. Again revolt flared, this time led by two figures who were to become legends for ages to come: the scholar "messiah" Akiba ben Joseph and the warrior Simon bar Kochba.[10] For three years war raged in the province of Judah until the arrival of the emperor himself and his ablest general, Julius Severus.[11] Slowly and methodically they swept the land, crushing all before them; but Roman losses were great. In his report to the Senate concerning the reconquest of Judah, Hadrian omitted the customary summation, "I and the army are well."[12] Bar Kochba, after occupying Jerusalem for two years, died at Roman hands in Bathar, a fortress southwest of the city.

Roman fury was great, and those Jews who survived the massacres of retaliation found their destiny stamped on the chains of Roman slave markets. The land lay in waste save for Jerusalem, which was a thoroughly pagan city peopled by Phoenicians, Romans, and Syrians. No Jew dared approach it on pain of death. Hadrian, like Antiochus Epiphanes before him, issued a series of edicts[13] making it a capital offense to follow the teachings of Judaism. But Hadrian did not stop there; he also forbade the teaching of the Torah and the ceremony of ordination which permitted it. In one blow he struck at the very heart of the religion he was determined to obliterate. A bloody purge ensued as eager Roman officials rounded up sages and students for public execution, a proceeding which brought favor from the emperor. The remnant of the Jewish intelligentsia, gathering secretly, decided on a division of laws into primary and secondary obligations, in an effort to curb the slaughter. Those laws pertaining to murder, idolatry, and adultery were held to be inviolable, while all others could be put aside by all but the rabbis, who, it was decided, should bear the full burden of the faith.[14] One of those was Akiba ben Joseph himself, who died under torture with the words of the Shema on his lips: "Hear O Israel, the Lord is our God, the Lord is One."[15]

In 131 A.D., to the great relief of Jewry, Hadrian died and was succeeded by Antoninus Pius.[16] Antoninus repealed the brutal edicts of his predecessor, except for those pertaining to the making of proselytes and the prohibition barring Jews from Aelia Capitolina. Schools were allowed to reopen and the Diaspora Sanhedrin founded by Johanan ben Zakkai once again cemented Palestinian Jewry together under the laws of Torah. This was the age of the *tannaim*, the scholars who finally compiled the oral traditions of Hebrew theology into the written code known as the *Mishnah*. The following centuries left Jewry to fend for itself, but a new force had entered the world in the ever-growing body of Christian believers.

These were years of radical change in the history of religions, as ancient ways fell before the tide of the new revelation. With the advent of Pauline theology, the fires of Christianity were lit and the new religion stood independent of its Jewish origins. The spread of the new faith was, in one sense, beneficial to the Jewish community, for the oppressive energies of Rome fell on the new church. Despite the persecutions visited upon them—perhaps even because of them—the Christian community grew rapidly into a major power throughout the empire. When in 312 A.D.[17] the general Constantine defeated Maxentius at the battle of Milvian near Rome, he quickly issued an edict proclaiming religious toleration. Now master of Rome, he moved against Licinius, emperor of the East, and by 325 A.D.[18] had taken the empire for his own. Seated on a throne of gold, Constantine presided over the famous Council of Nicaea[19] and observed the incorporation of Christian doctrines then under debate into the unified Nicene Creed, which became in that year the state religion of Rome. From the catacombs and gutters of the empire, the new faith rose to the highest possible station. The clergy assumed roles of great influence and moved quickly to impose restrictions on the Jewish community which had fostered them. Judaism in Palestine was again barred from making converts; and Jerusalem, now a city of splendid basilicas and churches, was once again forbidden on pain of death.

Between 361 and 363 A.D., the reign of Julian "the Apostate," ancient Roman religion enjoyed a brief revival as the state cultus; and Judaism had a respite from its oppressors.[20] At the emperor's expense, material was assembled in Jerusalem to rebuild the Hebrew sanctuary. The work, suspended because of a fire, was abandoned when Julian met his death during a campaign against Shapur II of Persia.

The Roman emperors who followed Julian adopted policies of religious toleration, but the Jews of Palestine found little comfort in them. They were barred from public office, forbidden to own Christian slaves (although, ironically, a Christian could legally own slaves), and forbidden to build new synagogues. During the reign of Theodosius II,[21] formal modes of social discrimination and rigid anti-Jewish measures were legally codified to facilitate enforcement and prosecution. Although the more liberal emperors endeavored to protect their Jewish subjects, local administrators learned quickly that it was more profitable to cultivate the favor of the local clergy. During the period known as the Byzantine Empire the choices open to non-Christians were conversion or oppression.

By the end of the fifth century, Rome was ruled by northern European "barbarians," leaving the emperor in Constantinople master only of Byzantium. As head of both church and state, the emperor had total power. Many of these rulers sought to crush all opposition to the church, and so the Jews suffered. Perhaps the most oppressive measures were those brought about by Justinian, who barred the observance of Passover until after Easter, required that Greek versions of the Scriptures be read in the synagogues and interpreted by Christian clergymen, completely banned the reading of Isaiah, and rigidly enforced the social bans of Theodosius II.[22] His *Corpus Juris Civilis*[23] fixed the legal status of Jews in Byzantine realms for 700 years to come.

Even when Justinian's immediate successors eased his rigid policies, the Jews were not yet at peace. The year 614 A.D.[24] found them rallying behind the neo-Persian monarch Chosroes II to rid Palestine of its Christian rulers and restore the Commonwealth. In the summer of that year the combined forces of Judah (under Benjamin of Tiberius) and Persia seized Jerusalem and killed 90,000 Christian[25] residents of the city. Churches and monasteries went up in flames as a long-oppressed people struck back with furied vengeance. For sixteen years Persian rule endured until the Byzantine emperor Heraclius conquered the neo-Persian empire in 630 A.D.[26] after making conciliation with his Jewish subjects. With Palestine once again in Christian hands, the monks and priests of the land demanded the extermination of the Jewish populace. The reluctant emperor was moved to act by Sophronius,[27] patriarch of Jerusalem, who proclaimed a week of fasting in preparation for the purge. Heraclius[28] proceeded to hunt down and massacre those who had helped him regain his empire. The only survivors were those who escaped to Babylon, Egypt, and Arabia. The days of Christian rule were numbered, however, for in the vast wastes of Arabia a new force was emerging that was to change the course of the world once more.

CHAPTER 3

The Rise of Islam

In about the year 610 of our era there appeared in Mecca, long a tribal center of the desert nomads, a figure who was to change the course of world history.[1] A camel driver by trade, this man called Muhammad had crisscrossed the deserts of Arabia, carrying goods from Yemen on the Arabian Gulf to Syria and the Levant. Perhaps it was while trading in the cities of Judea that he had first heard the words of the Shema: "Hear O Israel, the Lord our God is One." While he traversed the vastness of Arabia, he wrestled with the knowledge of God; as he did so, his mind filled with a zeal to bring to his tribal people the teaching of the oneness of God. It is told that in the fortieth year of his life, Muhammad received a vision, the last revelation of the Hebrew God spoken by the angel Gabriel. Rising to his prophetic office, the founder of Islam proclaimed, "There is no God but Allah!" a cry that was to reverberate for centuries from Gibraltar to Pakistan as the Arab tribes rose out of the desert to wage the Holy War with their response, "And Muhammad is the prophet of God!"

Displacing a well-established cult of over 300 separate

21

gods, however, proved a difficult task; and when the citizens of Mecca proved resistant to the new prophet, Muhammad fled northward to Medina. This was 622 A.D.,[2] the year of the great flight, or Hejira[3] (emigration), and to the future Islamic world it became the year one.[4] The largely Jewish population of Medina welcomed the fugitive, whose future, so he hoped, rested on their acceptance. After all, did he not descend from father Abraham and proclaim Islam (submission to God) in the name of the prophets of Israel? In those early years, converts were instructed to pray facing Jerusalem and were led by the prophet in observing the Holy Days of Judaism. In the second chapter of the Koran, he addresses himself thus to his Jewish brothers: "Children of Israel, remember the favors I have bestowed upon you. Keep your covenant and I will be true to Mine. Revere Me. Have faith in My revelations, which confirm your Scriptures, and do not be the first to deny them."[5]

It did not take long, however, for Muhammad to realize that the Jews would not follow him. They would, rather, oppose him as a false prophet. In a rage he proclaimed to his followers, "War is enjoined you against the infidels!"[6] During the seven years he remained in Medina, the prophet exiled or killed those who refused his call.

In 624, having rallied a sizable following, Muhammad seized Mecca, smashed the tribal deities that occupied its shrine, and proclaimed the oneness of God over the Kaaba, or sacred stone, of the tribal cult.[7] It is to this Kaaba that devout Moslems even today make their holy pilgrimage. The years that followed found the growing forces of the new faith making slaves or exiles out of resistant Jewish tribes, seizing their possessions and adding select widows to the prophet's harem. "God hath caused you to inherit their land, and their houses, and their wealth, and

a land on which you have not trodden."[8] In flagrant viola-
tion of the traditional desert code of warfare (for which the
prophet required a special revelation) Muhammad cut
down the date palms of the Banu Nadir, a Jewish tribe,
which he then starved into submission.[9] Such was the fate
of those who would halt his progress.

Eight years after the Hejira, Muhammad returned to
Mecca the master of Arabia and apostolic ruler of its
people.[10] Mecca replaced Jerusalem as the focus of Islam,
and the fasts and feasts of the Hebrews gave way to those
ordained by the prophet. In 632 Muhammad died,[11] and
so began the succession of the prophet in the office of the
caliphate. There began a rush of conquest, not known
since Alexander mastered the world, as the Arab tribes in
less than a decade subdued all the lands that lay within the
Fertile Crescent and continued for another century to push
west across North Africa and southern Europe. Many
Christians and Jews joined their Moslem conquerors in
smashing the power of neo-Persia and the Byzantine emperors. The Moslem rulers, on the whole, proved humane
masters. They divided mankind into believers and unbelievers, the latter being subject to certain taxes and civil
restrictions as well as religious prohibitions (i.e. restrictions against making proselytes), all of which proved
much harsher in theory than in practice.

Through the centuries that followed, the caliphate
underwent the upheavals known to every government,
and the center of power moved from Medina to Damascus
to Baghdad.[12] A partnership of sorts developed between
the Moslem authorities and their Jewish subjects, and
Jews eventually gained admission into the highest circles
of power and wealth in the empire. Learning flourished in
the academies of Babylonia that a few centuries earlier had
produced the Talmud. The Hebrew Exilarch (Prince of the

Captivity) was granted prestige and privilege in secular affairs, and the caliphate extended full religious authority to the Gaonim (heads of the Jewish academies).[13]

In Palestine it seems that the Jewish populace fared equally well. A thriving school rose in Tiberius, where, it is believed, the great liturgies of Judaism had their first flowering. There, too, developed the vocalization of the Scriptures (the Masorah). The Sanhedrin again deliberated the affairs of the community. The greatest strife endured by the Jews of the "homeland" was occasioned by repeated Byzantine incursions, which carried death and ruin in their wake.

In the intellectual atmosphere of the Diaspora, it was inevitable that schisms and sects should arise within Judaism. Messianic pretenders, mysticism, and radical schools rose to challenge the central stream of Jewish thought. And yet, despite the pressures of assimilation and divisionary trends, the Jewish populace flourished, the sacred ways of the fathers survived, and learning flowered. Such is one of the great ironies of history: out of bloody beginnings emerged centuries of relative prosperity under the dome of Islam. The community of the Eastern Diaspora flourished into the eleventh century, when, its great leaders gone and its prosperity waning, the focus turned westward to Spain. The zenith of Islam, at least in its original thrust, ended at about the same time that the Turks of Asia Minor descended on the Arab states to assume the central authority of the succession. Not until the reemergence of the Jewish state in our century does the East figure prominently in the course of Judaic affairs. The next burst of greatness was to occur at the opposite end of the Mediterranean, and there too was to begin one of the darkest hours of the Diaspora in Christian Europe.

CHAPTER 4

Western Jewry

The lot of Jewry in the lands of the Byzantine rulers was clearly difficult. Emperor after emperor openly harassed the "killers of Christ" through religious repression and civil discrimination. On the whole, the only laws of the state which were enforced on behalf of a Jew were those levied against him. And yet the major problem, as seen by the Christian rulers, was how to make Christians out of the Jews. Justinian's approach[1] (527–565) aimed at preservation of the civil status and religious practices of the Jews, but nevertheless relegated them to a position of social inferiority, thus making conversion an attractive alternative. Needless to say, he met with very little success. Leo III preferred a much simpler approach: in 722 he issued an edict ordering all the Jews in his realm to become Christians. The only effect his edict had, however, was to precipitate an exodus northward into the Crimea and the Caucasus.[2]

Since the days of the republic, Rome and the other great cities of the Italian peninsula had sheltered Jewish populations. The lot of these Jews was good as long as Rome paid allegiance to her pagan gods. With the coming

of Christianity, however, there came also official persecution and mob violence. The "barbarian" incursions of the
fifth century brought an end to the western empire and
ushered in Ostrogothic rule. These northern tribes were
"Christian," but they were Arian instead of Nicene; that
is, they denied the divinity of Jesus while adhering to the
ethical teachings of the faith. The Ostrogoth rulers followed a course of moderation in regard to the Jewish
populace, protecting them from the avarice of the bishops
of Rome. A century later, the Ostrogoths fell before the
armies of Justinian under the leadership of Belisarius;[3] and
the Jews who allied themselves with the Ostrogoths fell
victims once again to public persecution under the Code of
Justinian. In the meantime, the bishops of Rome had se-
cured supremacy in the lands of the western empire, and
their power encompassed civil as well as religious authority. Italy itself was in a state of decay. In 566 the Lombards
descended into the peninsula to wrest the greater portion
of it from Byzantine rule. Originally Arian by creed, the
Lombards embraced the Nicene orthodoxy, adding fuel to
the growing power of the bishop of Rome. Now designated as pope, the power of the church bishop spiraled
until in 774 he was able to drive out the Lombards with the
aid of his powerful ally, Charlemagne.[4]

　　The pattern of papal policy toward the Jew was, in
large part, the work of Pope Gregory I (590–604).[5] Although he wished to convert the Jews, he realized that this
end would not be met through force. He did deny them
the right to employ Christian servants or own Christian
slaves on the ground that it was not right for an infidel to
be the master of a true believer. His policies were not
always followed by his successors, though on the whole
the papal attitude was far more moderate than that of the
clergy, who, in the end, had the last word.

In the south of Italy, the Byzantines continued to hold
sway until 827, when the tidal wave of Islam finally overtook them. For two centuries the South Italian communities grew and prospered under Moslem rule.[6] Talmudic study and Cabalistic (mystical) lore flowered,
academies sprang up in Rome and elsewhere, and great
families rose to high stations once more. North Africa[7] too
saw a resurgence of Jewish influence. Alexandria in Egypt
was beyond doubt one of the principal centers of the era,
along with Fostat (near Cairo) and Fayum. Westward
along the coast, a major center rose in Kairwan near the
ruins of ancient Carthage. Close contacts were maintained
between these centers of Jewish life. As a curious messianic restlessness rose in the communities, stirred by tales
of kingdoms far north of the Alps[8] (the Khayars) and
south of Ethiopia (the Falashas)[9] peopled by Jewish tribes,
the Diaspora communities looked longingly eastward, but
to no avail.

Leading the Mediterranean world as the uncontested
stronghold of Jewish life was Spain. Local lore claimed
Jews had come to Spain after the destruction of the First
Temple (586 B.C.). At any rate, their arrival in Spain was
early enough so that by the fourth century their numbers
and influence were great enough to alarm the Christian
clergy. In 305 church bishops, meeting in council in the
city of Elvira,[10] adopted measures forbidding trade, inter-
marriage, or social contact between Christian and Jew.[11]
Unfortunately for them, the Jews lived in great harmony
with their neighbors; consequently, the dictates of the
clergy were largely ignored. Outside of the urban population, the rural inhabitants were still pagan. For the next
century the Jews of Spain flourished under Roman rule in
spite of the hostile clergy. In 409 the same wave of barbarian migration that was to topple Rome overtook Spain.

The first to appear were the Vandals, who swept south through Spain into North Africa and then went on to sack Rome. The next to come were the Visigoths,[12] of the same stock as the Ostrogoths, who were invading Italy. Like the Ostrogoths, these Arian Christians treated the Jews well—better, in fact, than they treated orthodox Christians, who were regarded as Roman allies and therefore enemies. The Visigoth rulers elevated many Jews to positions of great power and entrusted the northern defenses of Spain to Jewish contingents of the army, thus warding off Frankish incursions through the Pyrenees. For two centuries of Visigoth rule the Jewish community sank its roots evermore deeply into the soil of Spain. So strong did they grow that not even the centuries of persecution to come would be able to uproot them.

In 589 the pendulum began to swing against the Jews. In that year, the Visigoth ruler Reccared I embraced Catholicism,[13] an act which insured his crown as a divine sanction of the church rather than an elected office of the nobility, as was the custom of his people. Immediately Jews were forbidden to hold office, own slaves, intermarry, or even raise their own children (who were to be baptized by force). Fortunately, the nobility, finding the Jews too vital to harm, ignored the edicts of the king. Such was the price Reccared paid for the favor of the church. Reccared's successor, Sisebut, pursued a more severe course, posing as alternatives baptism or exile.[14] Many Jews submitted to baptism only to practice their faith in secret, while many others fled to France or to Moslem North Africa. The next century found the bishops of Spain steering their kings on a path of outright war against Judaism. Those caught practicing Judaism secretly were enslaved and their children sent to be raised in convents. King Euric[15] went further still, placing the Jews wholly at the mercy of the clergy and declaring their properties forfeit. His successor, Egica,[16] made all Jews slaves, confiscated their lands and properties, and seized all children age seven and above to be brought up by the church. In 701 Egica died, and as his son Roderic took the throne, Tarik the Moslem already occupied Gibraltar and was preparing to march into Spain. In July of 711, Tarik, with 12,000 Berber warriors, conquered the principal power centers of Spain in three days. Jews and Christians alike rallied to him, for Spain had fallen into chaos and corruption under the last several Visigoth kings.[17]

Persecution ceased, and apart from the usual Moslem tax[18] imposed on all unbelievers, freedom of religion was restored. In many ways, however, Islam had changed, and the new conquerers of Spain were more concerned with worldly successes than had been their predecessors in the Moslem world. In less than three years virtually all of Spain was firmly in Moslem hands. Cordova became the capital. The lot of the Jews again flourished, and they rose to share in the wealth and administration of the realm. For two centuries Moslem affluence grew, until, in 912, Abd-er-Rahman III assumed the title of caliph and ushered in Spain's golden age. The Jewish community shared greatly in the splendor of Moslem rule. Men of wealth and learning gained admittance into the highest offices of the government, and scholars, scientists, poets, and philosophers added the flavor of their Judaic heritage to the brilliance of the Moslem court. Assimilation, however, did not engulf them, for they lived in separate communities by choice and were granted fiscal and judicial autonomy by the caliphs. For five centuries the Jewry of Spain prospered; but as strife overtook the Moslems, it came also to rest on the Jews.[19]

In 1013, following a period of civil disorder during

which the caliphate fell apart, a new regime came to power in Spain. Under the new king, one Samuel ibn Nagrela (a Jew)[20] was given the title of vizier, an act unprecedented in Moslem history, for no infidel had ever before been so highly honored. Samuel was a man of exceptional ability, learned in six languages, and a warrior as well. His power was so vast that when his benefactor, King Habbus, died, the succession was determined by Samuel (known as Ha-Nagid or The Prince). A Jew actually placed the Moslem ruler Badis on the throne of Spain. Following Samuel's death in 1056, his son Joseph[21] assumed his duties; but, lacking the tact and wisdom of his father, Joseph incurred the bitter hatred of his Moslem subjects. In 1066, after a rumor had swept the city of Granada that Joseph was in conspiracy with an enemy prince, the long-jealous Moslems of the city seized the vizier and crucified him at the city gate. Next the Moslems turned on the Jews of the city and on December 30, 1066, massacred 4,000 in a single day. The incident, however, was just that, for the Jews of Spain weathered it unshaken; and their prosperity and good relations with the Moslems continued to grow.

Spanish Jewry was at the apex of its splendor. The great men are too numerous to even name, and it will have to suffice to say that what arose in Spain was an era of study and greatness that rivaled the brilliance of Babylonia. The twelfth century is "high noon," for it is the century of Moses Maimonides[22] and Yehudah Halevi,[23] among many others. But already the end was in sight, for the Christian reconquest of Spain had begun. Advancing slowly from the north, King Alfonso VI slowly gnawed at the Moslem provinces. His policy toward the Jews was to regard them as equals,[24] and he placed so many in high positions that he earned a reprimand from Pope Gregory VII.[25] The disunified Moslems found themselves facing disaster and quickly appealed to Yussuf,[26] king of the North African Almoravides, for aid. He came, he won, and he stayed. When Spain became a province of his kingdom, he bore down greatly on the Jews he ruled, for, being a new believer himself, his zeal for converts was very strong. Christian pressure continued to gnaw away at the Moslem centers, and the Moslem Berbers (also of North Africa) took the opportunity to overrun the stagnant Almoravides. By 1149 the whole of remaining Moslem Spain was under Berber rule. To the Jews they offered Islam or exile.[27] The tables turned, the Jews now fled for refuge to the Christian cities to the north, where they were treated with honor and allied themselves with the Christian ruler Alfonso VII. Under his rule, they prospered once more.

CHAPTER 5

Medieval Europe

The period just prior to those enigmatic centuries known as the Middle Ages found the Jews of Europe living in close cooperation with their Gentile contemporaries. So close was this interrelationship that the clergy of the period felt the necessity of indulging in anti-Jewish polemics in an effort to curb the rising influence of Judaism, which, in some cases, posed an outright threat to the church. The Archbishop Agobard, in the ninth century wrote:

> Things have reached a stage where ignorant Christians claim that the Jews preach better than our priests... some Christians even celebrate the Sabbath with the Jews and violate the holy repose of Sunday.... many of the people, peasants, allow themselves to be plunged into such a sea of errors that they regard the Jews as the only people of God, and consider that they combine the observance of a pure religion and a truer faith than ours.[1]

Jewish immigrants had come to Europe as early as the first century, following the Roman legions as they pushed into Gaul and settling along the frontiers. Communities along the Rhine grew and prospered until by the fifth century, when Clovis the Frank wrested what is now France and Germany from Roman rule, Jews were to be found spread throughout his realm. After Christianity became the state religion, certain social prohibitions were weighed against the Jews; but it seems they had little effect.[2] For many centuries to come the Gauls, Franks, and Jews lived in relative harmony, punctuated only occasionally by an overzealous ruler who sought to disrupt the good relations. In the early eighth century, Carolus (Charles Martel)[3] dethroned the last Frankish ruler in order to establish the Carolingian dynasty, which is best known in the person of Charlemagne (768 to 814). Charlemagne was a relentless converter, lashing out at the heathen on his borders in order to baptize them, but he appears to have left the Jews alone. Should a Jewish subject run into trouble, he had recourse to the "Master of the Jews," appointed by the emperor and charged with protecting Jewish interests.[4] The emperor's protection, however, was also of great benefit to himself, for Jews were the leading merchants and bankers in Europe; and as they prospered, so too did the king's coffers.

Charlemagne's son, Louis the Pious, pursued his father's policies concerning the Jews; and it was he who had to contend with the vociferous Agobard, archbishop of Lyon, who did not like seeing his flock converted to Judaism. Following Louis, the Carolingian empire fell apart; and we see the France and Germany of our day go their separate ways. The western Franks had become Latinized and spoke a Roman dialect which became the French of today; while their eastern brothers, too far removed from Roman influence, clung to their German dialects and customs. Neither country seems to have produced a strong leader, and what ensues is a period of anarchy and confusion which left the Jews at the whims of local lords. During the eleventh century, Jews were expelled from many French and German towns. The motive was often greed as opposed to religious fervor, for it was lucrative indeed to seize Jewish properties and commercial interests, a practice which benefited both church and state. Much of this activity had its roots in the "religious" zeal prompted by the call of Pope Urban II to the First Crusade (1096).[5]

In the summer of that year motley bands of social outcasts and misfits, led by the infamous monk Peter the Hermit, set out to recapture the sepulchre of Jesus, pausing along their way to attack Jewish settlements in Germany and France. Massacres and looting in some areas threatened the local lords, who, in many cases, came to the aid of the Jews at the risk of losing their own properties to the Crusaders. Faced with a choice of baptism or death at the hands of the Crusaders, many Jewish communities adopted the "tradition of sacrifice" Kiddush ha-Shem,[6] or mass suicide. These Jews were rumored to be legionaries of the Antichrist, born of demonic beings, etc.

The twelfth century saw economic life in Europe on the advance as a strong feudal system rose out of the decades of chaos. Trade guilds, from which Jews were barred, appeared in the cities. With commerce on an upward spin, credit operations quickly became essential; and since usury endangered the salvation of the true believer, the Jews of that day gained the clergy's endorsement to carry out these vital functions. This somewhat-forced occupation (seen as antagonistic by Christians), coupled with the stigmas of deicide and infidelity, brought the Jew into the forefront as a socially hostile "stranger." Secular rulers and church prelates were, in fact, invisible partners in the practice of usury, which, while adding to the Jews' antagonistic position, assured them of protection to a certain degree.[7] Thomas Aquinas summarized contemporary attitudes toward the Jew by stating that he was condemned to perpetual servitude for the act of deicide, but was not to be deprived of the necessities of life.

Each new call to a Crusade fueled anti-Jewish sentiment. With religious consciousness among the masses on the rise, the position of the Jew as a scapegoat for Christendom gained theological impetus. The Fourth Lateran Council[8] (1215) approved of the doctrine of transubstantiation, leaving Jews legally vulnerable to charges of host desecration. This Council also adopted a canon requiring every Jew to wear a distinguishing mark on his clothing (the "law of the patch"), a move aimed at further isolating the Jewish populace. Medieval sculptures and paintings depicted biblical patriarchs and prophets wearing the distinctive mark, and the Jews of the day were often represented as having horns and a tail. Contemporary literary references describe the *"foetor judaicus,"*[9] a peculiar smell possessed by a Jew, as opposed to the "smell of sanctity" possessed by a Christian. In fact, Jewish law required that a Jew bathe regularly, a practice not usually followed by non-Jews in the Middle Ages.

The thirteenth century saw the economic demise of the Jew, as the Florentine and Viennese banks of Italy and the Lombards in France rapidly took over the finances of the day. So far we have mentioned only the Jews of France and Germany. Considerable Jewish populations existed throughout Europe and England, and their lot had much in common with that of their brothers in Frankish realms. The Jews of England, as elsewhere, were regarded as the personal property of the king;[10] and if a wealthy one should die, the king would simply name himself as heir and seize the estate. This practice, widespread in Europe, aimed at maintaining the Jew in a servile position. With the advent of international banking, the English kings found they could dispense with their Jewish subjects, and in 1290[11] they ordered them to leave England. In 1306, an expulsion order was issued in France[12] by Philip IV. The Jews of Europe, condemned to roam from country to country peddling junk, forbidden to own property or land, provide us with the classic image of the Wandering Jew. Deprived of civil protection, target for every adventurer and vagabond, the outcasts sought refuge in remote provinces of Germany and in neighboring Poland, Austria, Bohemia, Hungary, etc. Yet their lot continued to decline. A strange paranoia crept over the lands of feudal Europe; a feeling of demonic conspiracy against God-fearing people festered in the minds of the masses; and the image of the Jew, spurned by God, spawned by Satan, loomed large in their nightmarish lives. Jews, it was said, poisoned Christian wells; their elders and rabbis suckled on sows and raped Christian wives. Jews, so some believed, killed Christian infants to obtain their blood for ritual use (the infamous blood libel, which led to the extermination of the Jewish community in Trent,[13] Italy, in 1475 and to the beatification of their supposed victim, the infant martyr Simon. Venerated until 1965, the cult was finally suspended by papal order). Jews also found themselves blamed for the devastating spread of the black plague.[14] These are some of the less colorful beliefs held during the Middle Ages.

The church, for the most part, condemned such popular libels, while maintaining the most ludicrous of all: the blood libel and the libel of host desecration. These charges, which led to the stake, are central to an understanding of the horrors of Spain's Inquisition courts. (It should be remembered that the libel was declared untrue in a papal bull issued by Sixtus IV,[15] but the belief was too widely held for even the Pope to curb.) The most hostile quarter as far as the Jew was concerned was the rising middle class. Formidable among these adversaries were the Franciscan and the Dominican orders.[16] Anti-Jewish uprisings racked European cities at the end of the fourteenth century. Poland, Spain, Italy, and Germany saw massacres and mob violence in the streets that clergymen and secular officials could do nothing to halt.

Throughout the fifteenth century the bloody tale continues. In the religious wars against the followers of John Huss (1419 to 1436) the Jews, accused of harboring and encouraging the Hussites, fell victim to slaughter and imprisonment.[17] In 1421, after a period of bloody uprisings, the Jews of Austria were expelled.[18] The same fate once again befell much of French and German Jewry. John of Capistrano in midcentury eloquently convinced Bavaria to expel its Jews, and Franconia quickly followed suit.[19] Franciscan colleagues of Capistrano, such as Bernardio la Feltic,[20] and the Dominican Vicente Ferrar[21] vehemently lashed out at the Jewish communities with charges of blood libels and insidious crimes committed against the church and against Christ. The Jews of Poland, long confined in ghettos, once again fell victim to mob violence.

Such were the centuries known as the Dark Ages, and to the Jews of that period the designation would have been appropriate, if not understated.

CHAPTER 6

The Inquisition and Expulsion of 1492

As our story approaches the period of the Renaissance and the Reformation, our attention is drawn once more to the kingdoms of Spain, where the last glimmers of Jewish life are about to be snuffed out. By 1265 most of what had once been Moslem Spain was back in Christian hands. Except for Granada and Cadiz, the rest of Spain's great centers once more had monarchs loyal to Rome. Loyalty, however, did not always extend into the realm of obedience, and for two centuries to come the Jews of Spain fared well under Christian rule. The kings found their Jewish subjects far too valuable to alienate, and throughout the thirteenth and fourteenth centuries the Italian popes had to repeatedly censure the Spanish monarchs for their liberal disregard of church laws concerning the Jews and for honors and favors bestowed on them. Despite this papal displeasure, Spanish Jewry prospered under royal tutelage and basked in a degree of communal autonomy comparable to that enjoyed under the Moslem rule. In return for this royal favor, the Jews of Spain supplied the king's coffers with huge sums of tax money, gathered and paid collectively, thus providing the monarch with a clear indication of their economic importance.[1]

The disaster which was about to befall them, however, was already raising its head in Spain. Following their successful eradication of the Albigensian "heretics" in France (13th Century),[2] the Dominican order was entrusted by the pope with the task of ferreting out heresy in Castile and Aragon (the two largest kingdoms of Spain). The institution through which their efforts were directed was the Inquisition, a complex system of investigation and trial which usually followed a pattern from informer to prison to the "rack" to confession, trial, and burning. At this point, Jews were not subject to the authority of the Inquisitors, for they were infidels, not heretics. Only after conversion, whether voluntary or forced, was a Jew answerable to the papal court. With growing zeal, the friars of Spain set about the task of "converting" Jews. When social isolation and degradation failed, edicts ordering conversion were employed. Yet despite the growing wave of opposition, the Jews of Spain managed to survive. They were too important in terms of wealth, influence, and sheer numbers to make it profitable for any but the foolhardy to attack or offend them. The years of the Black Death (1348 to 1349), which saw thousands of French and German Jews fall victim to the raging mobs,[3] found the Jews of Spain holding the upper hand against the rabble.

Intellectually, Spain's Jewry occupied itself in the pursuit of Cabala, meaning "tradition," a quest for the essence of man and his destiny which strove to uncover the secrets of nature and looked ardently for signs presaging the advent of the Messiah and the ultimate redemption of mankind. Strange messianic movements rose out of the Cabalistic teaching, and mystical schools sprang up to elaborate and perpetuate the quest for enlightenment.[4]

In 1371 the tide turned irrevocably against Spanish Jewry. In that year, Henry II seized the throne in Castile, ordering the immediate imposition of the "law of the patch"[5] and enforcement of other social prohibitions aimed at the Jews. The Jewish community fell into a state of decay. Living in forced segregation, the Jews sought to weather the storm, but this was not to be. In 1391 the growing storm broke first in the city of Seville.[6] The populace of that city stormed the Jewish ghetto from all sides, killing 4,000 and burning the area to the ground. Those who escaped survived by accepting baptism. From Seville the massacre turned northward to Cordova and Toledo and on into Aragon, Barcelona, Valencia, and Gerona. In the smaller communities, not a Jew was left alive. By the time the fury of death had spent itself, over seventy communities in Castile had been obliterated. The number of forced converts soared into the thousands. These new "converts" called themselves Marranos, meaning "the damned"; and so indeed they were. Some practiced their faith in secret, which led ultimately to the stake. Still, the worst was yet to come. The full power of the church was soon brought to bear on the Jews that survived. The ranks of the clergy swelled with apostate Jews, many of whom rose to high positions, a reward for their treachery. One in particular, a Paul of Burgos,[7] managed to persuade the Cortes (Parliament of Castile) to pass a series of laws making it a crime for a Jew to trim his hair or shave his beard. His clothing must be plain of cut and made only of the most inferior of materials (comparable to a gunnysack); he was forbidden to bear arms, engage in a profession or craft, or deal in wine, flour, meat, or bread;

and all debts owed him were declared null and void. The year was 1412. And yet Paul's zeal was not expended. At his invitation, the vehement Vincent Ferrar[8] was sent into the cities of Castile and Aragon on a crusade which netted him thousands of "converts." In Aragon, yet another force appeared in the person of Benedict XIII, none other than the pope himself, or rather the "antipope." (Since 1378 a line of dissenting "popes" had ruled in the French city of Avignon.)

Having lost his grip on the antipapal throne, Benedict sought to improve his lot by bringing about the conversion of all Spain's remaining Jews. To this end, he called the leading Jewish and Christian theologians of the day to the city of Tortosa, where from February of 1413 to November of 1414 the two sides disputed the merits of their respective faiths. Benedict's appeal was based, however, not on reason, but on fear. Those who were harassed into listening to the debates were confronted by a virtual army of bishops and knights. The keynote of the affair was sounded by a Dominican friar, himself a convert, who quoted from the prophet Isaiah: "If ye be willing and obedient, ye shall eat the good of the land; but if ye refuse and rebel, ye shall be devoured with the sword."[9] Vincent Ferrar provided a daily diversion by parading his converts in front of the assembly. A century and a half earlier, one Pablo Christiani had attempted a similar debate but failed.[10] Before long, it became apparent that Benedict too had failed. Like their counterparts of over a century past, the Jewish spokesmen made fools out of the almost-ignorant ravings of men like Ferrar and Benedict. Frustrated in his attempt at conversion, Benedict retaliated by convincing the government of Aragon to follow Castile's lead in imposing anti-Jewish legislation.[11]

For a brief period under the rule of John II (1406 to

1454) the Jews of Castile enjoyed a respite, for the king's deputy Alvaro de Luna[12] needed Jewish money and support in the timeless struggle between the nobility and the throne. Jews once again were received into government offices, and their autonomy was briefly restored. In Aragon, too, the times seem to have changed, and the Jews of that kingdom could breathe a sigh of relief. As John's successor, Henry IV (1454 to 1474), continued this relaxed situation, Jewish interests were on the rise once again. Had it not been for the presence of the Marranos, the disaster might have been averted.

Public indignation burned hot against the "new Christians," partly because they became too successful and partly because it was suspected that they practiced Judaism secretly. Marrano sons and daughters married into the nobility and even into royal families. It was not long before the situation came to be regarded by Spaniards of Gentile origin as an outright social invasion. Priests and friars saw heretics in all of them, even those who wore the habit of the church. With public fury kindling against them, in 1440 and again in 1467 the Marranos of Toledo were attacked by mobs. Six years later the same fate befell the Marrano residents of Cordova, Saen, and Segovia.[13]

In 1479 the piously conservative queen Isabella sat on the throne of Castile, and in that year the throne of Aragon fell by descent to her husband Ferdinand. With Spain now united under "the Catholic Sovereigns," the monarchs embarked on a policy of absolutism in domestic affairs and expansionism abroad. The nobility was stripped of all power, and in 1480 the royal Inquisition was ordered to stamp out heresy as treason to the state.[14] Marranos were herded to the stake, and even the dead did not escape. Bones and corpses were brought before the Inquisitor; and since these people had practiced Judaism in life, their re-

mains were now consigned to the holy flames. The properties of the deceased swelled the royal coffers. In 1483 the
Dominican monk Thomas de Torquemada,[15] already
inquisitor-general of Castile, was granted the same title for
Aragon as well. Thomas moved quickly to exercise his
power. Thousands of Marranos, confessing to heresy
"voluntarily," were stripped of their possessions and imprisoned for life. Those who refused voluntary confession
were tortured into confessing and summarily burned at
the stake. Torquemada employed the blood libel[16] to ferret
out Jews not subject to his court's jurisdiction, but this
method proved too slow. He decided expulsion was the
only solution; so on March 30, 1492, the Catholic
Sovereigns issued the infamous Edict of Expulsion,[17]
which brought down the curtain on almost a millennium
of Spanish Jewry. It is ironic that in that year Christopher
Columbus set sail for the West Indies on an expedition
financed and manned largely by Marranos and Jews.[18]
Columbus begins his diary by mentioning that he received
his commission in the same month that the Jews were
ordered to leave Spain.

From the Alhambra palace in Granada the grim news
spread that every Jew must leave Spanish realms by July
or choose between death and baptism. No gold or silver
could leave the country, although the sale of houses and
property was permitted. The real estate market became so
glutted that a large house with vineyards brought only a
cart and a donkey. In frantic last-minute attempts to nul-
lify the edict, Abraham Senior and Isaac Abarbanel, international financiers of vast resources, offered the king their
combined immense fortunes for the repeal of the edict. It
is related that the rulers began to waiver, when in came
Torquemada brandishing a crucifix before them, crying,
"Here! Take him and sell him!"[19]

To the end Torquemada maintained his efforts to force the Jews into baptism, but the great majority stood firm. With the words, "Let us go in the name of the Lord"[20] on their lips, some 300,000 Jews set out for nowhere.

Many of the exiles crossed the border into Portugal, where they bought permission to remain for eight months. Many were ultimately sold into slavery. Four years later those who did not choose death were forced into baptism. Thus a large body of Marranos came into existence in Portugal, and their fate followed the same course it had followed in Spain.[21] In 1506, 2,000 of them died at the hands of a mob. In 1531 the Inquisition overtook them. Many fled to the New World as well as to the far reaches of the Old.

In the year 70 the Diaspora began with a great wave of westward migration. Reaching England, it was turned back in 1290, from France, in 1394. In the ghettos of Germany it lay decaying, and in 1492 it was sent eastward once more out of Spain. Throughout the lands of Israel's exile a cry of agony rose as the Jews of Spain plodded eastward. Gone was the only glory the remnants of the Hebrew state had known since the Second Temple fell.

The year 1492 is one of the momentous turning points in our story. We shall follow the twice-exiled Jews across Europe and the lands of the Reformation and see them come to rest once more in Moslem lands.

CHAPTER 7

Moslem Turkey and Reformation Europe

The roads eastward from Spain led invariably through the states of the Italian Peninsula. To Sicily, as well as to the duchies in the north, the Jews of Spain found their paths marked. Over the centuries the lot of the Italian Jews had fluctuated dramatically; but with the constant chaos that typified the duchal principalities in the north, when life became unbearable in one state, these Jews could find refuge in a neighboring state until times changed for the better.[1] For generations the flux of events had found German Jewry buffeted back and forth between Italy and their homeland, but never before had there occurred an influx as great as that created by the expulsion from Spain in 1492.

So it was that while Niccolo Machiavelli penned his philosophy of statecraft, an invasion of outcasts swept into Italy. While it is true that these newcomers were exiles and for the most part stripped of their possessions, they

47

nevertheless brought with them the skills and traits which had made them great in Spain. To the communities of Italy they brought a new burst of life. The Jews of Italy were not lax in their responsibility to their brothers in faith; and for those who fell into the hands of the slave traders, the ports of Italy promised ransom and freedom.[2]

In the great cities of Italy the Renaissance had dawned: learning, art, and music blossomed after the long winter of the "Dark Ages." Hand in hand with this rediscovery of the arts of culture came an interest among certain members of clergy in the Hebrew language and in the vast amount of Judaic literature it could unlock.[3] It is this interest that added to the rising atmosphere of change which was soon to burst forth into the Protestant Reformation.

Throughout the fifteenth and sixteenth centuries the lot of the Italian Jews rose and fell in rhythm with the political upheavals of the day. A curious messianic fervor grew among the communities, especially among the bitterly oppressed Marranos of Portugal, when a dark-skinned messenger from the East, David Reuben, appeared in Rome in 1524 with a plan to ally his Jewish ruler with the monarchs of Europe in a war against the Turks. For a brief time, it appeared that his plan would succeed, but in the end he met death at the hands of the Holy Roman Emperor Charles V.[4]

Against the precarious mosaic of Italian life shone the rising splendor of the Ottoman Empire to the East. To this shining haven of refuge came millions of Jews to share in the prosperity of the Moslem rule. During the sixteenth century, Salonika and Constantinople harbored the largest Jewish communities in the world.[5] The Jews proved to be loyal and valuable subjects, and against the occasional avarice of a pasha or a governor, the sultan and his officers offered protection. Once again the exiles made their presence known in high places. Bayazid II[6] eagerly opened the doors of his empire to the Jews of Spain. Joseph Hamon[7] served as physician to Bayazid's successor, Selim I. Joseph's son Moses served as physician to the almost-mythical Suleiman the Magnificent.[8]

The Ottoman rulers were quick to recognize the great benefit which could ensue were they to shelter the exiles, especially those of wealth and position. So it was that when the Venetian Republic imprisoned one Gracia Mendes,[9] widow of a powerful Portuguese banker, the sultan's government pressed for her release and the restoration of her properties. When her retinue arrived in the Turkish capital, she was accompanied by her nephew, Joseph Nassi.[10] A man of learning who understood the complex European diplomatic labyrinth, Joseph soon won the sultan's favor and served him as a valuable advisor. Suleiman gave Joseph the city of Tiberius in the Galilee as a refuge for his people. Joseph quickly issued a call for Jews of the Diaspora to return to their homeland. Ships were dispatched to carry the immigrants, and hundreds of Jews suffering bitter persecution in the papal states responded. Joseph rebuilt the city and tried to establish a silk industry, but the experiment failed.

Under the rule of Selim II, Suleiman's successor, Joseph's importance gained international scope. Dukes and kings came asking him favors, and yet he was soon to meet his match. The man who eventually supplanted Joseph at court was a brother in the faith, Solomon Ashkenazi.[11] Solomon came to the sultan's service from the court of King Sigismund Augustus of Poland, bringing an impressive record of achievements and a battery of diplomatic skills.

The intrigues of court life, however, stand in sharp

contrast to the quiet life of a small town in Galilee, known as Safed. In terms of intellectual activity, this tiny village overshadows the glory of the sultan's court, for it was there that Isaac Luria[12] founded a school of Talmud and Cabala, which gave rise to the mystical system that bears his name. His disciples carried his speculations and his messianic contemplations throughout the lands of the Diaspora, where they took root and flowered as a major force (albeit one secondary to the mainstream) in Jewish thought.

In the Christian West, too, the winds of change were rising. As learning flowered, so did the spirit of reform; and it was not long before the time-honored ways of the church came under scrutiny. In Germany, Martin Luther rose to challenge the authority of the Catholic church. For the first time the Bible was translated into the vernacular and made available to the masses. Quickly the newly-accessible canon became the most powerful influence in propagating religious reform.

Beginning in 1509 a bitter controversy raged through Europe as to the place of Judaic writings: were they worthy of study, or should they be consigned to the flames? Johann Pfefferkorn[13] and the powerful Dominican order championed the latter position while the German scholar Johann Reuchlin[14] and the Franciscans took the former. Pope Leo X vacillated, fearing the powerful Dominicans but leaning toward Reuchlin. After years of politics and intrigue, the Holy See and Leo X ruled in favor of Pfefferkorn, not so much out of opposition to Reuchlin and his pro-Judaic stance as out of fear of Luther, whose cause had gained powerful support from Reuchlin's followers.[15]

The success of Luther's reforms infused the ghettos of the Diaspora with a spirit of messianic expectation. Could such earthshaking events signify less than the advent of the Messiah? At first, Luther himself took a most sympathetic attitude toward the Jew. In an early pamphlet, *Jesus Was Born a Jew,* he declares:

> Our fools, the popes, bishops, sophists and monks, these coarse blockheads, dealt with the Jews in such a manner that any Christian would have preferred to be a Jew. Indeed had I been a Jew and had I seen such idiots and dunderheads expound Christianity, I should rather have become a hog than a Christian.... I would advise and beg everybody to deal kindly with the Jews and to instruct them in the Scriptures; in such a case we could expect them to come over to us.[16]

Luther's expectation is clear enough: a purified Christianity must succeed in attracting the Jews.

In his later years, however, a bitter and battle-scarred Luther, reversing his position, lashed out with brutal vehemence at those who professed the Jewish faith. In a series of blatantly anti-Semitic pamphlets, Luther offered new advice for Christian conduct regarding the Jew. In his *Concerning the Jews and their Lies,*[17] he advised his followers to eradicate Jewish homes and synagogues by burning them to the ground and covering the site with dirt; prayerbooks and Talmuds were to be destroyed, rabbis silenced on pain of death, travel forbidden, wealth seized, and usury stopped; young Jews were to be enslaved at hard tasks. As a final step, Luther advocated expulsion: "Let us drive them out of the country for all time." He concluded, "To sum up, dear princes and nobles who have Jews in your domains, if this advice of mine does not suit you, then find a better one so that you and we may all be free of this insufferable devilish burden—the Jews."

Historically, the churches who followed Luther also followed the tone of his later advice.[18] On the other hand, the followers of John Calvin[19] maintained a more hospitable stance regarding the Jew. The great role played by the Old Testament in Calvin's writings led the Puritan sects to identify themselves with the Jews of the biblical narrative and thus to respond favorably to contemporary Jewry.[20] The French Calvinists, a somewhat special case, maintained an outright pro-Jewish position, for they were brothers in persecution until the reforms of the French Revolution.

The immediate consequence of the Reformation was to distintegrate the lot of Jews in Catholic lands.[21] With the advent of the Counter Reformation and its zeal to restore ecclesiastical authority, the theses of Augustine and Thomas Aquinas were employed to the letter; Jews were confined in locked ghettoes and rendered servile, being permitted only such prerogatives as were considered necessary to maintain life.[22]

Erasmus stated at the beginning of the sixteenth century: "If it is incumbent upon a good Christian to detest the Jews, then we are all good Christians." The eighteenth-century French publicist G. B. Roberti expressed an equally ironical sentiment: "A Jewish ghetto is a better proof of the truth of the religion of Jesus Christ than a whole school of theologians."

CHAPTER 8

Jewry in Poland — The Sabbatian Heresy

The decades surrounding the Reformation movements of the sixteenth century found European Jewry, and that of Spain in particular, subjected to a new form of harassment. For the sake of clarity let us state that the Jews we are speaking of are those designated as the "new Christians" or "Marranos": Jews who chose baptism over death and exile and so came into the fold of mother church. Since 1492 no Jew dared raise his head in Spain, but a considerable number of Marranos were still residing in Spanish realms. Against the possible "Jewish threat" these new converts posed, laws were created making "purity of blood" (limpieza de sangre)[1] a criterion for barring the entry of those of Jewish descent into various guilds, and military and religious orders. This blood sanction was soon extended to include admission into universities and military academies. The law was strictly enforced under the rule of Emperor Charles V. Anyone

53

suspected of having Jewish ancestry was subjected to a detailed genealogical search. Thus the religious anti-Semitism of past centuries was transformed into outright racial Judeophobia.

Against the turmoil of European society in the six-teenth century, a new haven of refuge was found in the principalities of Poland. To the cities of Cracow, Lublin, Warsaw, and other towns and villages too numerous to name the Jewry of Europe came. There the academies of Talmud and Torah flourished; and there, despite rigid legal controls, the Jewish community achieved a level of autonomy surpassing that of Spain or even Babylon. The Vaad Arba Arazoth (Council of the Four Lands)[2] presided over the affairs of Polish Jewry with full legal and religious authority. In authority, the Vaad has been compared to the ancient Sanhedrin, the major difference being that it was more directly representative of the common people. Its members appointed "agents" to the Polish Diet and court, levied taxes, regulated business transactions, and labored to improve relations with the Christian commu-nity. Important as these functions were, the greatest con-cern of the Vaad was the education of the young. It is a timeless testimony to the Jewish spirit that in an age so intellectually stagnant it was almost impossible to find an illiterate Jew anywhere, no matter how destitute or op-pressed. Throughout the rest of Europe, only the clergy and high nobility were able to read or write. Consequent-ly, it should come as no surprise that throughout the lands of their dispersion Jews rose to positions of intel-lectual as well as political power and wealth. So, too, in Poland.

In 1572, the Polish monarch was rendered powerless against the whims of the nobility by a constitutional provi-sion known as the *liberum veto*.[3] This veto enabled a single member of the Diet to block legislation by pronouncing the phrase "I do not permit." Needless to say, the Diet was not a model of efficient government. Less than a century after the institution of its constitutional government, Poland faced a grave crisis; and unfortunately, the decay that plagued the Diet had stripped her of her brilliant statesmen and generals. A brief example will serve to illustrate: In 1643 the Diet, in an effort to suppress Jewish business interests, set the legal profit margins for Christian merchants at seven per cent, while the Jews were to be limited to three per cent.[4] It did not occur to the nobles that they had, in effect, put the Christians out of business by forcing the Jews to undersell them.

In 1648 the crisis[5] erupted as Poland's Cossack subjects (nomads occupying the borderlands on the Dnieper River) rose in revolt against the Polish gentry whose land they worked, the Jewish middlemen who administered the land, and the Jesuit Order which had long persecuted them for their Greek Orthodox faith. In 1635 and 1636 they had rebelled unsuccessfully, at which time they lost their autonomy and privileges. A fierce hostility grew between Cossacks and Poles, and in the middle stood the Jews. Almost all contact with the Polish gentry was through the Jews, who collected taxes, acted as merchants, and (because of a move by the Jesuits to humiliate the Cossacks) administered Greek Orthodox Churches. Aware of their perilous position, the Jews relied on the Polish nobility to protect them, but in 1648 they learned that their trust was ill-founded. In that year, the Cossack hetman (chieftain) Bogdan Khmelnitski, allying himself with the Tartars of the Crimea, inflicted a massive defeat on the Polish Army. Jews in Cossack lands were stamped out. By the time Poland recoiled and stopped the tide of death in 1651, hundreds of thousands of Jews as well as Poles had been killed. For three years "peace" endured; but during that time the Cossacks transferred their allegiance to the Czar of Russia, and in 1654 massacre swept into Poland once more.[6] Again the Jews suffered the consequences of generations of distrust, and now the wrath of the Judeophobic Russians was added to the raging hatred of the Cossacks. One year later, Charles X of Sweden marched into Poland from the north. This time the invader was a Protestant. Charles did his part to reduce the Jewish population in the north; but since he stopped short of the horrors the Muscovites and Cossacks were inflicting in the east, the Catholic Poles concluded that the Jews had conspired with him. As the Swedes retreated, the Poles lost no time making up for Charles' shortcomings. In the districts of Posen, Kaliz, Piotrokov, and Cracow, Jews were annihilated and their synagogues given to the Dominican Order. By 1660 when the fury began to abate, some half-million Jews, representing 700 communities, had been killed.[7] Despite their most valiant attempts, the remnant of Poland's Jewry was never able to raise its head again.

During this period known as the "Black Decade," the Jews of Turkey continued to flourish. In the city of Smyrna, a young student of the Zohar and Lurianic Cabala named Sabbatai Zevi[8] proclaimed, in 1648, the ineffable name of God, speaking aloud the holiest word in the Hebrew tongue: YHWH or Jehovah. Tradition held that only after the Messiah had come could this act be performed, and Sabbatai next proclaimed that it was he who was, in fact, the long-awaited Redeemer. So began a movement that swept the lands of the Diaspora in a whirlwind of enthusiasm, concomitantly provoking stiff opposition. For twenty years the "Messiah" and his followers traveled the lands of exile proclaiming the advent of Israel's restoration which was to occur (so it was believed in some circles) in the year 1666. Powerful and wealthy men followed the young "Redeemer"; even philosophers and scholars were counted among his adherents. In Cairo he married a Jewess named Sarah, who had escaped imprisonment in a Polish nunnery. In 1665 Sabbatai and his bride returned in triumphal procession to his native city of Smyrna. The momentous year 1666 was at hand; and throughout the ghettos of Europe—London, Amsterdam, Hamburg, Venice, Warsaw, and Rome—the outcasts prepared for their glorious triumph. In the spring of 1666, the entire Jewish population of Avignon, France, sold or gave away their real properties and waited for the moment of glorification of their "Lord." Sabbatai and his retinue set sail for Constantinople in the spring of 1666 amid an air of jubilation. There, it was believed, he would realize his messianic office. Sabbatai was, instead, imprisoned in the fortress of Abydos in the Dardanelles. Strange as it may seem, this apparent setback only added to his power, and pilgrims flocked to see him. His prison became known as *Migdal Oz,* the "Tower of Strength," and from it Sabbatai held court like a monarch. As his "prophets" spread the news of his "glorification," the fervor continued to mount; so too did the opposition.

A self-proclaimed Polish prophet, called Nehemiah by his followers,[9] declared the advent of the Messiah but refused to name Sabbatai. Summoned to Abydos, Nehemiah would not capitulate and fled to Adrianople and the sultan's court. Once safely in Turkish hands, the prophet threw down his mantle and became a Moslem, convincing the sultan's advisor that the Sabbatian movement was a plot to overthrow his ruler. After various avenues of action were considered, it was finally decided that the sultan's physician, himself a Jew turned Moslem, would go to Abydos and attempt to convince the "Messiah" of the truth of Islam. He succeeded; and in a shattering move Sabbatai entered the sultan's presence, proclaimed the faith of Islam, and took the name Mehemet Effendi. So much for the glorious restoration of an oppressed but hopeful people. Confusion and despair spread; still many refused to abandon their faith, preferring to believe the conversion was a necessary part of Sabbatai's mission. The "Messiah" fostered this belief by proclaiming "God has made me an Ishmaelite" and embarked on a double course, teaching Cabala to Moslems and Islam to Jews. In 1676 the "Redeemer" died in exile in the town of Dulcingo in Albania.

For another half century the Sabbatian heresy spread into even more bizarre sects, following reincarnations of the "Redeemer." Sometimes the opposition from mainstream Judaism erupted in violence, and it was not until 1756 that the last flickers of the strange phenomenon died out.

Instead of deliverance, the already destitute communities of the Diaspora were dealt a spiritual blow. Out of the turmoil came further decay, materially as well as spiritually, for to poverty was added the plague of discord among brothers. Very few Jews were left in the upper stratas of European life, the majority existing in the shadowy borderlands of society. True, there were still great men of wealth and learning, humanitarians and men of power who recalled Jewish roots; but their numbers were few and the relief they were able to offer was small. As our story enters the eighteenth century, the Jews of the Diaspora found themselves at a low ebb. Although they did not know it, brighter days lay ahead. A new intellectualism was rising in Europe that was to open the window on the musty European society and infuse it with a new naturalism and humanism which was to have a broad and enduring impact on all of western civilization.

CHAPTER 9

The Enlightenment

As the breath of reform swept through the institutions of Western society, a new intelligentsia arose in Europe which fulminated against the oppressive dogmatism of the "dark" centuries. The movement claimed to derive its substance from nature, not law, and thus came to be known as *natural philosophy*, the force underlying the period we know as the Enlightenment. It was a school of thinking which stressed justice and human dignity, humanity, virtue, and tolerance. This new class of bourgeois thinkers denounced Christianity in the name of Deism (natural religion) and stressed equity in human rights. Throughout the centuries of undisputed church domination in Europe, the Jew could exist only in the shadows of society, occupying a position shot through with prejudice and suspicion. With the advent of the Enlightenment and the dawn of modern secularism, the humanistic movements of the eighteenth century began to batter down the walls which for centuries had isolated the Jewish world from the Christian world.

Advocates of the movement, who called themselves the "philosophes,"[1] labored ardently to remake society based on logic and reason. Among the great scholars are found the names of Voltaire, Montesquieu, Lessing, Rousseau, Diderot, and Kant, to name but a few. Theirs was a task of monumental proportion, and the impetus of their thinking was to push mankind into the technological age. Aside from the academic rigors they encountered in the course of their work, they had to contend against centuries of stagnant social ideals and ecclesiastical bureaucracy.

The Jews became a subject of rigorous concern, for not only were they the most oppressed people of the century, but also they held the dubious distinction of being the supreme target of Christian intolerance throughout history; and this intolerance the Enlightenment was sworn to destroy. Across the Continent in the spoken word and on the printed page, the "philosophes" preached that Jew and Christian share alike in a common humanity and thus in a common cause of human rights. These eighteenth-century men for the most part did not yet foresee the emancipation of the next century. When, in 1791, the Jews of France were granted equality before the law,[2] it was largely the authority of the Enlightenment thinkers which ultimately overcame the powers of church and Gentile economic interests.

It has been suggested[3] that despite valiant efforts to save the Jew from persecution, the Enlightenment sought, in actuality, to exploit his plight in order to discredit Christianity. It was therefore not humanism but politics that led to the concern for Jewish rights. The men of the Enlightenment chose to espouse the cause of Judaism for reasons of their own, treating Jews not as individuals but abstractly as an incident of outraged conscience. The pre-

dicament of the Jewish community was used to demon-
strate the faults of Christianity, whereas traditionally it
had been employed to testify to its truth. As a result of this
third-person regard for the Jew, the Jew as a human being
was still viewed with suspicion and distaste. In the final
analysis the Jewish faith, like the Christian, was to the
Enlightenment a superstition and thus was something to
be eliminated. Because of its particular nature, Judaism
was regarded as antisocial; and the end of emancipation
was not the acceptance of it, but its conversion into something compatible with the majority culture. So widespread
was this view that when in 1791 the revolutionary government of France granted Jews full citizenship, it felt
compelled to state that while they were entitled to full
rights as citizens of the state, as Jews they counted for
nothing in terms of any contribution to its life.

More outright anti-Jewish sentiments flowed from
the pens of Diderot, Holbach, and Voltaire.[4] Their polemics surpassed the rational bounds of criticism and certainly
fell short of the great standard of reason. Vicious and hateful as these attacks were, they must be seen in context.
Although the three men just named were the most viru-
lent anti-Christians of the day, at the time they were at-
tacking Judaism it was still very dangerous to denounce
the church outrightly. By abusing the Jews in print instead
of the Christians, these writers could escape prosecution
and still pour scorn on Christianity for its undisputed
Jewish origins. The tactic itself, however, does not fully
account for the hostility such literary abuses fostered.
Prejudice against the Jew still ran hot in the veins of the
masses, and of course much bitterness arose in response
to Jewish economic successes made possible by the emancipation movements. These sentiments were, to be sure,

masked in the magnificent rhetoric of literary genius and came off sounding like carefully thought-out sociological treatises.

Voltaire, whose detestation for the Jews was unequalled, pressed his argument to suggest that Jews were ignorant by virtue of their very nature, incapable of making social adjustments, and therefore a hindrance to social harmony and progress. He contended that the juxtaposition of the Jew and modern society was seemingly irreconcilable. If such arguments sound vaguely familiar, it should be remembered that the weapons of bigotry are limited and timeless. If a tactic works once, it is used again.

Fortunately, the racist overtones of certain elements of the movement had little effect on the overpoweringly egalitarian mood of the Enlightenment. Diatribes against the Jew, even those of Voltaire, appeared more in the nature of emotional excesses than of serious moves against them. The impact that such sentiments had was of a subtle nature. Perhaps unknowingly, the Enlightenment writers had changed the course of anti-Semitic thinking and set it on a new path. "Intellectually" sophisticated, their criticisms of Jewish life and thought provided the emerging modern world a new stage on which to air its animosities. What developed was a secular racism proffered in the name of overriding social aims. It was willing (even eager) to assimilate the Jew, if only he wouldn't act like a Jew. What we have, then, is the reemergence of the most ancient theme in anti-Semitic feeling: the concept of the Jew as a peculiar alien element, resistant to the pressures of society, unyielding in his thinking, and unwilling to accept the "benefits" of assimilation.

In the past, such statements may have contained elements of truth, but the centuries of oppression had weighed greatly on the Jewish community. With the avenues of access back into the mainstream of society opening before them, the reformist sentiments of Europe began to find their way into the Jewish world.

Moses Mendelssohn of Berlin, coming to the forefront of the community, launched a vigorous and unrelenting campaign for cultural blending. Of the Gentile world, Mendelssohn demanded absolute equality for his people; of his own constituents, he asked that they learn the language and absorb the culture of Gentile Europe (particularly German culture). Rising to become one of the luminaries of the German intelligentsia, he counted among his friends some of the greatest men of the day. Ephraim Lessing,[5] poet, dramatist, and critic, immortalized his own admiration for Moses in the play *Nathan the Wise*. Immanuel Kant, too, was counted among Mendelssohn's friends. In 1763 Mendelssohn won a philosophical essay contest in which Kant was one of the competitors. Frederick II of Prussia was so impressed by the victory that he "elevated" Mendelssohn to the position of "protected Jew."[6] In 1767 a work on the immortality of the soul *(Phaedon)*[7] won him further acclaim. Written in impeccable German literary style, the book was translated into many languages and became a best seller.

In 1770 the thrust of Mendelssohn's work turned back to the Jewish community. He translated the Pentateuch and the Psalms, as well as the commentaries and prayers of his people, into German. For many, this effort provided an avenue of escape from the center of bitter controversies, for his approach placed the Scriptures (so it was held) on the level of great literature.[8]

In the field of equal rights the battle was strenuous. It was an era of enlightened rulers, and Mendelssohn and his followers made headway in many areas, winning the repeal of anti-Jewish acts still operative since the Middle Ages and the opening of schools and universities to students of Judaic background. His work won him both acclaim and condemnation, for it was feared that the new educational opportunities would lead from the ghetto to the baptistry.[9]

Mendelssohn himself remained a Jew in the truest sense of the word. Faithful to his heritage, he declared that if the price of freedom was denial of the Jewish faith, he would not pay it. His influence, however, did have the opposite effect. Of his own six children, four accepted baptism. The imprisonment of the ghetto was overpoweringly intolerable in the face of an enlightened free world. The dream of Europeanization that spurred Mendelssohn on seemed destined to come into being. The question that remained was whether or not the stampede out of the ghetto was the beginning of the dissolution of Jewish life.[10]

> Once in a while, I take an evening stroll with my wife and family. "Papa," one of my children asks innocently, "What is that fellow over there yelling after us?" "Yes, Papa dear," another speaks up, "They always follow us in the street and call us names. They cry 'Jews, Jews!' Do they think it bad to be a Jew? Why else would they keep away from us?" Alas! Averting my eyes, I sigh to myself: "Man, oh, man, is this what you have finally accomplished?"[11]

CHAPTER 10

The Age of Revolution and Its Aftermath

The year was 1786, and in a remote new country a constitution was being drawn up that would serve as a model for a new era of political change. In Article Six the founders of the American Republic declared: "No religious test shall ever be required as a qualification to any office or public trust in the United States." In 1789 the Constituent Assembly of France in its "Declaration of the Rights of Man and of the Citizen" picked up the refrain, declaring: "Men are born and remain free and equal in rights . . . . no one shall be molested on account of his opinions, including his religious views." The following year the Americans added an amendment to their documents of state stipulating that "Congress shall make no law respecting the establishment of religion or prohibiting the free exercise thereof."[1]

So it was that the light of hope burned once more for the disenfranchised and oppressed peoples of the world.

To the Jews of the Diaspora, the news of emancipation resounded with an intensity of joy similar to that which must have accompanied the giving of the law, for now for the first time in centuries Jews would be free to follow that law in the tradition of their fathers.

A new epoch had begun in the history of nations, and the people who had suffered for generations under the old order were not the last to mark time with the new. To many, equality before the law seemed like the dawn of the messianic age; but the lessons of history had been too harsh for such notions to long endure. From the New World came a cry for freedom, a call to revolution. To the millions of Europe's exploited masses it was long overdue. When a French queen faced with a hungry mob cried, "Let them eat cake," the mob responded by leading her to the executioner. The tumult which went hand in hand with the revolutionary movements of the eighteenth century is well known. As the walls of monarchy crumbled, what was left in its wake was often worse than what had gone before. And yet, out of such stormy beginnings was to emerge a new, "modern" world.

The influence of Hebraic thought underlying the revolutions, particularly the American Revolution, has gone for the most part unnoticed. In a total population of roughly three million, the Jewish community in revolutionary America numbered only three thousand. From the timeless traditions which this small group of people represented were drawn the cornerstones of the new republic. The Puritans, whose leadership in New England fostered the climate for change, operated from an Old Testament theology.[2] Contemporary preachers expounded Old Testament themes and concepts which coalesced into the motto "Rebellion to tyrants is obedience to God." Jefferson, Franklin, and Adams proposed that this motto be inscribed on the Great Seal of the United States, a seal that was to bear an image representing the Exodus of Israel from Egypt.[3] From the Book of Leviticus came words so expressive of the hopes and aspirations of a nation that they were chosen for the inscription of the Liberty Bell: "Proclaim liberty throughout the land unto all the inhabitants thereof."[4]

In spirit as well as in form, the American government drew heavily on the model of a Hebrew commonwealth;[5] and so frequently was the comparison made that many came to regard the new country as an Israel reborn. Statesmen and educators, clergymen and artisans, laborers and farmers, all along the eastern seaboard of the young republic were well aware that the mantle of state they were lifting from the dust of history had been borne before by another people, who had covenanted together to form "one nation under God."

On August 17, 1790, the Jewish congregation of Newport, Rhode Island, delivered an address to be presented to the first President of the United States:

> Deprived as we hitherto have been of the invaluable rights of free citizens, we now (with a deep sense of gratitude to the Almighty disposer of all events) behold a Government, (erected by the Majesty of the People) a Government which to bigotry gives no sanction, to persecution no assistance, but generously affording to All liberty of conscience and immunities of citizenship.... For all the Blessings of civil and religious liberty, which we enjoy under an equal and benign administration, we desire to send up our thanks to the Ancient of Days.[6]

In reply Washington wrote:

> It is now no more that toleration is spoken of, as
> if it was by the indulgence of one class of people that
> another enjoyed the exercise of their inherent natural
> rights.[7]

It has been said so often as to forebear repetition that equality cannot be legislated, and so it was in the new republic. In 1784 attempts to make Christianity the state religion in Virginia were defeated.[8] Maryland did not abolish its prohibitions against the Jews until 1826.[9] North Carolina[10] and New Hampshire[11] both had laws restricting Catholics and Jews from holding office; laws which were repealed, however, in 1868 and 1877 respectively. No change can ever be made effective without time being allowed for it to take root.

In France the emancipation was hard fought, and it was not until 1791 that the provisions of the Constitution were clearly defined to include the Jews.[12] The institution of the Republican calendar which provided for worship in the "Temple of Reason"[13] left the Jews in a suspect position, for they could not participate in such practices, even though the practices were nationalistic rather than sacramental. Their defenders against charges of antirevolutionary activities were many and powerful, including the champion of the Reign of Terror, Robespierre himself.[14] By July, 1794, the revolution entered a new phase, signaled by the adoption of the Constitution of the Directory. With France at war with the most powerful monarchies of Europe, the armies of the Republic required decisive leadership. French Jewry hurried to bear arms in defense of their land, and the wealthy among them poured their assets into the battle as well. The armies of the Republic left France, taking with them the liberating ideals held in such repugnance by the vested interests of Europe's nobility. To the upper strata the French brought conquest; to the millions of impoverished peasants, freedom.

When in 1798 the French took Rome and held Pope Pius VI a prisoner of war, the Jews of that city exploded from the ghetto and joined arms with their deliverers.[15] In 1799, when the French retreated, the new Pope, Pius VII, herded the Jews back into the ghetto.[16] Germany, although not engaged in active conflict with France, refused the pressures of humanitarianism and maintained its sanctions against the Jews.[17]

November of 1799 found the Directory abolished and one man standing with the reins of power: Napoleon Bonaparte. Before seizing power in France, Napoleon, while engaged in an ill-fated effort to conquer Egypt, issued a call for the Jews of Asia Minor to join him in driving the Turks out of Palestine. Their reward was to be a restoration of the Jewish state.[18] When his call went unheeded, he was forced to retreat; but the suggestion itself shows the monumental degree of equity (even though it was politically motivated) at work during the period. Not since the pall of Diaspora fell upon the Hebrew people had such a proposal been made by a force potentially capable of accomplishing it.

At Austerlitz on December 2, 1805, Napoleon crushed out the last vestiges of the Holy Roman Empire. Then at Jena, on October 14, 1806, he broke the back of the Prussian states and brought Poland into the French column. What both had refused to yield to the cause of justice, they now were forced to accept as the price of conquest. Emancipation followed the French armies like a shadow; however, vestiges of the old restrictions lingered on for lack of adequate measures to enforce their abrogation. The Prussians, stunned by their losses, hurried to soothe their newly-aroused consciences. By 1812, reform had reached the Jews and they were free of all legal prohibitions except for that banning them from the government.[19]

The farther east the tide of revolution swept, the stiffer the social opposition grew. The prejudices and practices of centuries past still held great sway, and even when legally prohibited, the old ways refused to die.

Following the defeat of Napoleon and the subsequent reordering of Europe, the progress of emancipation slowed. The Congress of Vienna, in redesignating the boundaries of nations and deciding rights of sovereignty, ostensibly upheld the freedom of the Jewish community. What happened, however, was quite another matter. Economic and social restrictions were revived, and in Germany nothing short of disaster ensued.[20]

In 1819 the cities of Germany rang with the cry "Hep, hep!"[21] as students and merchants mounted a war of national fervor against German Jewry. The origin of the phrase is unknown, a popular explanation holding it to be the first initials of the Latin phrase *Hierosolyma est perdita:* "Jerusalem is destroyed." It was first used, supposedly, by the maurauding crusaders of the eleventh century, and reechoed by their cultural heirs in the nineteenth.

The Jews of the Bavarian city of Wuerzburg would have perished like their ancestors had it not been for their well-organized defenses. The pogroms soon spread until all of Germany was embroiled in nationalistic anti-Semitism, for it became popular ideology that Jews were an alien element in German culture, an element which prevented Germany from realizing its destiny as master of nations. Poets, philosophers, historians, and theologians took the Jews to task in expounding the new myths of German superiority. Not even the vastly powerful Rothschilds escaped mob fury; and although men like

Goethe and Schleiermacher publicly derided the Jews, not one influential voice was heard in their defense.

The course of eighteenth- and early nineteenth-century anti-Semitism was the most ancient and deadly of all. *Xenophobia* (fear of strangers) placed the Jew in an alien light. The end of emancipation was seen not in acceptance per se, but in assimilation. When in the course of time this did not occur, the Jew was left standing in the spotlight of society like a freak. Old prejudices overcame the spirit of humanism; and, although the Jewish community enjoyed legal freedom, its social interactions were barred by the collective force of individual bigotries. Fears ran so rampant and wild that in 1807 the French author Abbi Barruel in his *Memoire Pour Servir A L'Histoire Du Jacobinisme* "revealed" a plot organized in that year by Jewish leaders attending the "Great Sanhedrin" in Paris (a meeting called by Napoleon to discuss the assimilation of Jewry into French society), which, it was purported, aimed at world domination. Barruel's work is the ultimate source of all subsequent references to the myth of the Elders of Zion.[22]

As the nineteenth century opened, the battle for emancipation had suffered major defeats. Old hatreds had flared up once more, and the struggle to realize the promise of freedom had to begin anew.

CHAPTER 11

Germany in the Nineteenth Century

The emancipation movements of the eighteenth and nineteenth centuries brought new freedoms to the Jews of Europe, but with those freedoms came a backlash of resentment and renewed antagonism. With a rapid expansion of industry and commerce brought about by an explosion of technical advancements in every aspect of society, the very nature of that society underwent some fundamental changes. Capitalism reared its head in the marketplace, and to those who understood its potential for profit it brought great fortunes. It was an age of new ideas and new ways; it made and ruined lives and was at once invigorating and unscrupulous.

Secularization was the vogue of the "sophisticated" as men rushed to pay homage to their own achievements and heaped scorn on those who still clung to the "cumbersome" theologies of the past. Some among the Jewish community, too, joined in the spirit of the age by adopting Christianity as a socially-inoffensive doctrine which they hoped would ease the stigma of their Judaic heritage. Reform and Conservative movements arose within the Jewish community in response to the stampede out of the synagogue; and, modeling their rites after those of the church, Jews picked up the refrain, "Assimilate! Assimilate!"

Despite such dramatic attempts at acculturation, the gulf between Jew and Gentile remained. Among the lower classes, where many found themselves at the wrong end of the capitalistic hierarchy, resentment waxed hot. Victimized by the rapid rise of the new prosperity, the exploited masses sought a scapegoat; and they did not have to look far. Among the newly-prosperous businessmen and entrepreneurs, who stood out more clearly than the Jew?

Since the publication in 1844 of the essay *On the Jewish Question* by young Karl Marx, the path had been cleared for the association of the spirit of capitalism with the Jew. (It should be remembered that "capitalism" was not yet a popular phenomenon.) Max Weber placed the origin of capitalism in the camp of Protestantism, where, from a practical point of view, it properly belongs.[1] Against this view Werner Sombart voiced the opinion that it was the Jew, not the Protestant, who was the historical progenitor of capitalism.[2] His work, published in 1911, traced this capitalistic spirit back to the biblical narrative. The leading German historian of the period, Heinrich Treitschke, lashed out at the Jews from yet another quarter.[3] Riding a crest of nationalistic sentiment, he held the view that the newly-emancipated Jews (who considered themselves thoroughly German) were still an alien element obliged to destroy their objectionable identity and vanish into German society. Indeed, Germany was the primary cauldron of anti-Semitism throughout the century; and yet this small antagonism was not even a shadow of what was to come.

Class conflict, coupled with the equation of "Jewishness" and capitalism and nurtured by a growing awareness of national identity, formed the basis of anti-Semitism in Germany—and, with slight differences, in the rest of Europe as well. We must remember, however, that this seed of hatred was yet a seed, a minor irritant to a people basking in the newly-acquired light of freedom. Neither the Jews of Germany, nor Jews of any other nation, for that matter, could foresee how deadly a seed it was.

German anti-Semitism began as an outbreak of peasant resentment against the Jews, who, according to the peasants, were determined to destroy their way of life through exploitation and contamination. The year was 1819, and the rhetoric was, at best, medieval. The resurrected hatreds, however, soon gave way to nationalistic reactions to the Napoleonic Wars, which were, in turn, tempered by the romanticism which swept Europe at the end of the hostilities.

In Germany these forces combined into an expression at least superficially noble concerning the German spirit. Rising out of Teutonic forests, this spirit of a people was an organic and eternal identity to which they alone could lay claim.[4] Richard Wagner elevated such poetic myths into the realm of art through his operas. And, just in case anyone failed to catch the full implication of the credo, he forcefully declared that the Jew was, of necessity, excluded from the quasi-religious brotherhood of the German heritage. Added to this elitist attitude was the argument (originally the work of Gobineau)[5] that race determines all; this implied that the Jew, being Oriental rather than Aryan, was by nature different. The German

interpretation equated *different* with *inferior*. Fast on the
heels of such thinking, Houston Stewart Chamberlain
(Wagner's son-in-law) published *The Foundations of the
Nineteenth Century* (1899), in which he carried the fore-
going beliefs to their logical conclusion: the presence of
Jews in German society was a detriment and inimical to
the progress of German ideals (namely, to German unity).
Still, the seed had not yet sprouted.

The main thrust of liberal German political thinking
regarded anti-Semitism as reactionary, and even the leftist
socialists would not swallow the pretense that all Jews
oppressed the working class. These were middle-class
people, the very people who had made possible the Jews'
entrance into society; and they were not quite ready to
admit that they had been wrong. The Jew, on the other
hand, was never really regarded as German, even in
friendly circles. He was a symbol, rather, of the "universal
rights of man," which every civilized country clamored to
recognize. His advancement in German society was, then,
that of a universal man, not that of a son of the land.
Rising out of the ghettos into the ranks of the middle class,
most of the Jews of Germany found themselves in the
unfortunate position of being in direct competition with
their benefactors.

As the century progressed and the potential hazards
of competition with the Jews became more apparent, the
German middle-class began drifting to the right politically. By midcentury, as the romantic conservative movement gained impetus, the spirit of liberalism that once
pervaded Germany had substantially faded. By the late
nineteenth century, anti-Semitism had become politically
acceptable, and was widespread enough to afford its advocates a distinct, although contrived, advantage. The Jew
was pictured as non-national, successful, rich (yet unpro-

ductive), foreign, powerful, exploitative, etc. We must remember that it was in Germany in 1879 that Wilhelm Marr first coined the phrase "anti-Semitism."[6] In that same year, Adolph Stoecker[7], head of the Christian Socialist Party, made one of the first modern public speeches expressing blatant anti-Semitism. His party then embarked on a campaign based largely on an anti-Jewish platform. Such hostility was, fortunately, not long-lived, for toward the end of the century movements of social reform came temporarily to a halt. A new kaiser ruled a united German state, and with his rule came a prosperity and a sense of security that superseded the need to employ the Jews as a national scapegoat. As far as social acceptance was concerned, however, the gulf remained. A dangerous myth lay smoldering beneath the surface of German national life. In one short generation the world would learn just how dangerous it was.

CHAPTER 12

Czarist Russia

The nineteenth century, as we have seen, witnessed a new and dangerous turn of affairs. Jews of Germany became the target of nationalistic anti-Semitism, and to a lesser degree so did French Jewry, as a result of the famous Dreyfus Affair. Farther to the east, in the countries of Central Europe and czarist Russia, such state-led anti-Jewish activity was far worse. Western Europe was, after all, at least theoretically committed to the doctrines of emancipation. In czarist Russia, the situation was quite different.

After the partitions of Poland in 1772, 1793, and 1795, the greater part of Poland's Jewish population[1] found itself thrust under the scepter of Czarina Catherine the Great. This turn of fate was unfortunate indeed, for Holy Russia had never forgotten the almost "disastrous" fifteenth and sixteenth centuries,[2] which saw nobles and even priests of the church converting to Judaism. Since that period, the official policy of the Russian crown had been to deny Jews the right to so much as live within the borders of the third "Rome" of the North. The policy was, of course, hardly enforceable; but the attitude it engendered can be seen in the reply of Empress Elizabeth (1741 to 1762) to a petition to allow Jews to immigrate to Russia. "From the enemies of Christ I desire neither gain nor profit."[3] Such pious royal disfavor can be traced to the very beginning of the Russian monarchy, and beyond that into the courts of Byzantium. The absolutism with which these policies were pursued derived its validation from the Greek Orthodox theology; and so deeply ingrained was this theology that every czar to sit on the throne of Holy Russia considered it his sacred duty to protect the Russian people from Jewish economic interests, indeed even from the presence of Jews in their midst.

To the Jewry of Poland, Russian rule brought renewed nightmares. Taxes levied against them were exactly double those paid by Christians. In 1791, the first of many edicts was enacted against them: the edict defining the "Pale of Settlement."[4] According to this official pronouncement, Jews were restricted to specially-selected provinces of the empire, and a line of military vigilance barred entry to the rest of it to all but a privileged handful. By 1808 the policy had been extended to bar Jews from villages within the Pale, forcing them into a few congested urban areas, where they came into competition with the Christian merchants. Ruin and disaster followed the beleaguered community as it was herded around Poland, and it was in the end only as tax collectors and agents of the bureaucrats in Moscow that many of them survived.

Catherine the Great was succeeded by her rebellious son Paul I, whose five-year reign ended in assassination. During his reign, Jews became the object of his official, although highly suspect, concern. The nobility ultimately triumphed in convincing him that it was the Jews, not themselves, who were responsible for the dire condition of the peasants.[5]

Following Paul there came to the throne a "reformer," Alexander I, whose reign aroused great hopes. In 1804 he inaugurated a statute commonly known as the "Jewish Constitution,"[6] which aimed at nothing short of total metamorphosis of the Jewish populace. Of paramount importance to the scheme was that the Jews were to become farmers, and to this end two more provinces were added to the eleven comprising the Pale. Public schools and universities were opened to Jews, and they were permitted to open schools of their own, provided Polish, Russian, or German was adopted as the official language. The statute, which was very thorough, prescribed a complete change of occupation, language, dress, and social habits. To achieve the desired end of creating a new class of tillers and planters, the czar's forces herded the Jews out of the rural areas into the major cities, driving them like cattle into public squares where they were left to fend for themselves. It was hoped that since they would be unable to support themselves in the cities, they would migrate into the countryside. Unfortunately, the government had failed to provide adequate facilities to accommodate them in their new occupation. Branded a dismal failure by the official committee appointed to oversee the affair, the expulsions were stopped. In a surprising move, the committee announced that the government, and not the Jews, was to blame for the program's failure.[7]

The "Grand Army" of Napoleon made its entry into Russia about the time the czar's program was abandoned. Jews, instead of rallying around the banner of emancipation offered by the French, chose to fight with the Russian armies, for they feared the undermining of their heritage which freedom might bring. Their service was rewarded with a favorable official attitude, and many of the preposterous provisions of the Jewish Constitution were rescinded. But Alexander was not through with them yet.

Following the Congress of Vienna, the duchy of Warsaw was ceded to the czar—and with it came an influx of Jews. Napoleon had been stopped, and out of the countries the French had occupied the Congress carved a new Eastern Europe.

Alexander, however, had taken to mysticism and became somewhat of a fanatic about it. Out of his visions emerged the "Holy Alliance": Russia, Prussia, and Austria. The rulers of the three lands swore to rule with love and fatherly concern, despite the fact that their union operated as an ironhanded instrument of oppression. The czar became filled with a zeal to convert the Jews of his empire, and to that end he became a member of the "Society of Israelite Christians."[8] In 1818, at the conference of European powers held in Aachen, Alexander laid out a plan for the conversion and the subsequent emancipation of Jewry. The conference humored the czar but did not adopt his proposal.

Much to Alexander's chagrin, the wave of influence seemed to be moving in a direction opposite to what he had hoped for. Judaic influence once more flowered, as a sect called the "Sabbatarians"[9] (adhering to Jewish rites) grew dramatically. In 1812 the sect had won government recognition, but in his old age Alexander sought to suppress it. Thousands of the sectarians were exiled to Siberia and the Pale, and in 1824 the old policy of resettling the Jews was again revived. Alexander, despite all his good intentions, proved incapable of grappling with the "problems" his Jewish subjects put before him; and yet, tumultuous as his reign was, it was like a confectioner's delight compared with what was to follow.

Alexander's successor, Czar Nicholas I, was personally responsible for the enactment of more than half of all the 600 laws concerning Jews enacted between 1640 and

1881. One Russia, one language, one religion—these were the aims of the "Iron Czar." As an autocrat he knew no rival, and he bent himself to the task of destroying Judaism as a distinct cultural entity.[10]

In 1827 his government instituted the "cantonist"[11] system for the conscription of army recruits. Technically, a cantonist was a soldier's son, the property of the state, and therefore born to fight. Nicholas imposed the system on the Jews of his empire with merciless cunning. Each community had a quota of conscripts, and if it failed to meet it, the officials responsible for filling it became subject to conscription themselves. The difference between the old cantonist doctrine and the new was that whereas the old applied only to soldiers, the new was aimed at Jews. Children were torn from their homes and exiled to camps in remote provinces of Russia for periods of twenty-five years. The aim of such drastic measures was simple: baptism. Few who resisted conversion survived, and over half of the conscripts never even got to the camps. Youths who sought to escape the compulsory service were hunted like animals. Since the communities were constantly unable to fill their quotas, there emerged a professional regiment of kidnappers preying on the children of the Pale. While the law required that the conscripts be twelve, the "chappers," as they were called, were not so discriminating. Little boys were torn from their homes; and of the thousands taken, very few were ever seen again. Life in the camps offered two possibilities: baptism and active army duty or torture. Regarding the latter, Hitler's armies could have taken lessons from their Russian predecessors.

On the economic front, Nicholas moved to destroy the Jews. In 1835, the "Statute Concerning the Jews"[12] was adopted. This statute collected the old laws regarding the Jews and added new ones to them. As the Pale was narrowed, old anti-Jewish restrictions were tightened and resettlement was attempted once again. In 1844, at the behest of his Minister of Public Instruction, the czar created a system of crown schools[13] designed to aid in the process of Russianizing the Jews. This project received sympathetic support from Jewish intellectuals at home and abroad, but the common people wisely distrusted the czar's intentions. Despite inducements and pressures, the Jewish community saw the schools for what they were: an outright attempt at wooing the children of the Pale from their heritage.

The czar met this resistance with even heavier taxes and renewed expulsions. Efforts to intervene from the West fell on deaf ears. When Sir Moses Montefiore was sent as personal envoy from Queen Victoria to the czar, he was met with the respect due him, but on his departure he was wholly ignored.[14]

With the outbreak of the Crimean Wars (1854–1856) a new avenue of conscription was employed: upon presenting Jews without passports (the great majority) for recruitment, the captor was granted immunity from service.[15] The corruption and social cannibalism of this system can be readily imagined. Nicholas died while the war still raged, making his son and heir "Autocrat of all the Russias."

Alexander II (1818–1881) spent the first ten years of his reign reforming the Russian government and society. The peasants were officially freed from their centuries-old serfdom, the cantonist system was abolished, provincial assemblies were established, and the judiciary was reformed.[16] As the Pale was slowly expanded, access into the heart of Russia was granted to an ever-widening class of Jews (soldiers, merchants, artisans, dentists, etc.). Alexander clung to the crown schools until in 1873, when, admitting their failure, he ordered them closed.

As times changed for the better, the spirit of enlightenment reached into Russian culture. In the universities,[17] as the political changes of the West were studied, a restlessness began to grow. Jewish intellectuals preached assimilation[18] in the Pale; and some went out with a newer message: a call for revolution. Secret societies were formed to prepare the peasants for the coming of a new order; and although the Jewish members were few, it should be no surprise that the most-oppressed people of the empire would rally to the cause of social change, convinced they would not be passed by. When reform movements led to demands for a democratic constitution, a few looked hopefully toward a socialist republic.[19] Those whose political bent leaned toward socialism called themselves *nihilists;* they countered the czar's suppressive moves with a program of terrorism. In 1863 revolt broke out in Poland. Coupled with unrest in Russia, this new antagonism sent the czar and his government into a spin of reactionism.[20] Fearful of the Russian people, Alexander resorted to the ancient practice of finding a scapegoat; and the Jews won.

In March of 1871, a pogrom swept the city of Odessa, the most cosmopolitan center in all of Russia. A policy[21] of blatant persecution and official criticism was adopted against the Jews in an effort to stem the tide of social unrest and the growing force of revolution. Realizing his attempts had been futile, Alexander later determined to put an end to the chaos by the most drastic of measures: a move toward representative government. On March 13, 1881, Czar Alexander II signed a decree ordering sweeping changes[22] in the government. Shortly after doing so, he went for a drive near his winter palace in St. Petersburg and was assassinated by the very forces he had hoped to appease.

The following day Alexander III reversed his father's decree and embarked on a course of total absolutism: autocracy, supremacy of the orthodox religion, and compulsory Russianization. The reactionary press quickly, and wrongly, fixed the blame for the czar's assassination on the ranks of Jewish radicals. The new czar, seizing the opportunity for a scapegoat, adopted a plan to solve the "Jewish problem": one-half of the Jews would be baptized, one-half would be starved to death. Standing at the czar's right hand was his master planner, Konstantin Pobedonostsev, the procurator of the Holy Synod (next in importance to the czar as head of the Russian church). The pogrom had become an official government policy.[23]

Only six weeks after the new government came to power, a wave of murderous pogroms swept the land. In 160 towns and villages Jews were killed and their property pillaged. Although it is doubtful that the government was directly responsible, it certainly stood in a position of passive approval. To the defense of the terror-stricken Jews came priests and Russian peasants alike, and in the fall of 1881 the horror subsided. What was demonstrated was the power of the czar, not the animosity of the people, for in general Jews and their Russian neighbors were on friendly terms. It was, rather, the rabble who, assured of official protection, exploded into a frenzy of murder and looting. The world responded with cries of outrage. In an attempt to exonerate itself, the Russian government declared the pogroms the "harmful consequences of the economic activity of the Jews for the Christian population."[24] At the sham "trials" which followed, the prosecutor exhibited his government's feelings by denouncing the victims rather than accusing the criminals. After Great Britain, France, and the United States responded with appropriate diplomatic protests, the czar was forced to yield to world opinion; but his course was still firmly set.

On May 3, 1882, the so-called "May Rules"[25] were enacted; and the "cold" pogroms began. While ostensibly guaranteeing protection, the laws prohibited Jews from settling or purchasing new land in the Pale and imposed mandatory closure on Jewish merchants on Sunday and on Greek Orthodox holidays. Phase two of the great plan had begun; and Jews by the hundreds began streaming across the Russian border looking for some sort of escape. To many, America became a land of refuge. With the enactment of the "closed number"[26] law, the number of Jewish students permitted to enter high schools and universities was severely limited. Again, as a stampede to western Europe began, the czar smiled at his success. In 1889[27] Jewish law graduates were prohibited by imperial decree from the practice of their profession. Expulsions involving tens of thousands of people swept through the great cities of Moscow, Kiev, and St. Petersburg.

Notable efforts, both diplomatic and philanthropic, were undertaken to aid the beseiged Jews of Russia, but all failed. A physician named Leon Pinsker[28] issued calls from Odessa for a second Exodus. "Let us," he wrote, "obtain dry bread by the sweat of our brow on the sacred soil of our ancestors!"[29] Societies sprang up all over Europe and in the U.S., and in 1882 three settlements were established in Palestine, populated by Romanian and Russian exiles. After Baron Edmond de Rothschild threw his enormous assets into the project, others soon followed. These were the BILU[30] settlers, a name compounded from the Hebrew initials of the phrase "House of Jacob, come and let us go!"

Still, the vast majority of Russia's Jewry remained.

They had nowhere to go and no way to get there if they had.

In 1894 Alexander III was succeeded by a man whom history will long remember: Czar Nicholas II, the last of the princes of Moscow. In his hands lay the fate of six million Jews, the largest Jewish population in the world. To the world's dismay, he announced in January of 1895 that he would ardently pursue the policies of his father; and to that end he retained his father's ministers. The Jews of the Pale had been dragged so low that all that remained was for him to stamp on them, and stamp he did. Pogrom followed pogrom, as Jews were slaughtered in the streets by czarist agents known as the *Black Hundreds*.[31] Nicholas made no secret of his membership and support; indeed, it was his official policy to "drown the revolution in Jewish blood."[32] Unfortunately, it was too late for poor Nicholas to do so.

Like Marie Antoinette, who cried "Let them eat cake!" Nicholas resounded with "Give them more blood!" In 1911 the charge of ritual murder was levied by the czar's government against Mendel Beilis[33] of Kiev. His acquittal followed two years of bloody riots and enraged international protests. Holy Russia was in a turmoil of war on every front. In 1917 the curtain fell when Nicholas II, last of the Russian czars, died at the hands of revolutionaries. For a brief period in February of that year, liberal humanitarian factions of the many revolutionary groups within Russia came briefly to power, and Jews apparently would have been granted the rights of full citizenship[34] had these factions held onto the government. Russian leaders on the whole, however, were at best divided on the question of anti-Semitism; even the great Tolstoy[35] was not always quick to come to the defense of Jewish people. Lenin,[36] an opponent of anti-Semitism, insisted nevertheless that the Jew more than the Russians must undergo a drastic change.

The situation to this point can be summed up in one word: hopeless. One famous observer of the plight of Russia's Jewry is said to have asked continually, "How do you bear it?" It was August of 1903; the man was Theodore Herzl.[37]

CHAPTER 13

America and Europe Before World War II

The last quarter of the nineteenth century witnessed what could be called a third Diaspora. Not since the fall of 1492 had so many Jews been on the move. The inhuman deprivations suffered in the lands of Eastern Europe had reached the point of intolerability. Thousands of the beleaguered millions poured into Germany and the states of the Austro-Hungarian Empire. For many, Western Europe was the end of the line; but to those fortunate and adventurous enough to brave the journey, an even brighter light shone ahead. To the port of New York the victimized refugees came, flocking to a land that held out the promise of peace and prosperity. At the outbreak of the Civil War the Jewish population in the United States is estimated to have been roughly 200,000.[1] From 1881 to 1920 the rate of immigration rose to a virtual flood. Eastern cities swelled with German, Romanian, Polish, and Russian Jewry, responding in spirit to the words of Emma Lazarus, which were to find their place in the American conscience at the base of the Statue of Liberty:

Give me your tired, your poor,
Your huddled masses yearning to breathe free,
The wretched refuse of your teeming shore,
Send these, the homeless, tempest-tost, to me,
I lift my lamp beside the golden door!

Over two million[2] Jews came to the United States in the greatest tide of immigration known to history, for the overall influx of "refugees" from 1881 to 1920 reached a figure in excess of twenty-two million.

The new immigrants moved quickly into all areas of commerce, for the era was one of expansion and prosperity. Education became a prime objective as first-generation sons and daughters reached up into the higher levels of American social life. The problems faced by the newcomers were paralleled only by those of the more established Americans who were their neighbors, for the newcomers were old-world people transplanted into a social climate quite unlike what they had known. As a result, clanlike neighborhoods developed, where the "alien" could find comfort and security among his own countrymen. As new ways moved in to replace the old, the transition continued; and the process of melting down many nationalities into a conglomerate American identity evolved into a systematic pattern of progress up the social ladder.

To the aid of this huge new labor force came the unions,[3] in a period of our economic history perhaps best characterized by conflict and not a small degree of chaos. From the Old World had come socialistic revolutionary ideals which were being applied to the masses of factory workers and common laborers with much difficulty, for many of these ideals were not consistent with the contemporary American society. From the strife and din of controversy, however, was to emerge a giant and conservative labor movement, the American Federation of Labor. Socialistic doctrines faded into insignificance and the newly-naturalized union members were quick to be caught up in the potentialities of the two-party system. Jewish leadership in the labor movement is a well-known fact; and while even in our own decade the role of the unions is still a source of controversy, it must be admitted that the unions helped immeasurably in integrating a vast number of workers into the mainstream of American life. Among the Jewish immigrants, the garment industry became the chief avenue of entrance into the new prosperity, and the labor movements which rose among them coalesced into the Amalgamated Clothing Workers of America, International Ladies Garment Worker's Union, and others.

Language was, of course, a major hindrance to the newcomers, as it had been in the Old World as well. Fortunately, the Jews of Eastern Europe shared a common tongue in Yiddish, and it was not long before newspapers, novels, theater plays, and commentaries appeared in the vernacular of the immigrant community.[4] Such avenues of communication proved to be blueprints of what was to come, for the Yiddish press taught the new arrivals the history and customs of their adopted land, preparing them for their role in the American cultural amalgam.

Anti-Semitism was nonexistent in the United States for the first two centuries of its settlement. Following the adoption of the Federal Constitution, those remnants of prejudicial laws still on the books were systematically erased under the provisions of the new document. It was not until the tidal wave of immigration of the late 1800s and the early 1900s that the age-old conflicts began to appear. The first symptom was the battle for property and neighborhoods as the lower-income "natives" were displaced by the very foreign Jews of eastern Europe. As the newcomers began to put down roots, their ancestral drive for learning sent them flocking into the colleges and universities in numbers disproportionate to their own in relation to the overall population. As a result, the institutions imposed unwritten quotas,[5] establishing a fixed number of positions to be filled by Jewish applicants. Discrimination in housing as well as in social clubs and certain public facilities soon followed, and resistance arose to Jewish endeavors to enter the fields of heavy industry, insurance, and banking.[6] What must be emphasized, however, is that the Jewish immigrants were not alone during that reactionary period following the mass immigrations, nor did they for the most part succumb to what resistance they encountered.

Prosperity came to Jew and Gentile alike, and with it some of the class-oriented conflicts disappeared. Not until the Russian Revolution and the disastrous economic collapse known as the Great Depression did overt anti-Semitic sentiment become public. Once again the weight of blame fell on the Jew,[7] perhaps because he was so closely associated in the American mind with anticzarist sentiments and the field of finance. The emergence of the German-American Bund[8] in the 30s pushed the issue still further, so that under the demented influence of Nazism the "cause" of anti-Semitism advanced. For a brief time it looked as if those rumblings against the Jewry of America might take a serious turn, but with the outbreak of World War II the public ground swell subsided as America faced a real and truly dangerous adversary.[9]

While it is true that the seeds of democracy and the ideals of equitable freedom had come from the Old World, it was only in the New World that they were to fall, at last, upon fertile soil. Although the great moves toward emancipation that began in the universities of Europe brought about the abrogation of centuries of restrictive laws, the social prejudices these laws engendered would not easily die. In 1867 the Ausgleich[10] guaranteed equality to the Austro-Hungarian Jews; in the early 1880s the German government of Otto von Bismarck made similar promises;[11] in 1858 Jews were admitted to the British Parliament[12] without the stigma of restrictive oaths; and in 1871 the Italian Risorgimento[13] ended the papacy's rule of that country and abolished the rat-infested ghetto of Rome. Emancipation had dawned in Europe, and the Jews were quick to act. The vernacular tongue replaced the Yiddish of the ghetto, and in social customs as well the Jewry of Europe became thoroughly European. Yet even assimilation was not enough; distrust and suspicion stalked the Jew into the modern age, and the timeless curse of anti-Semitism once again rose to haunt his life.

Germany, as we have seen, was the breeding ground for modern Judeophobia, and in no small measure Otto von Bismarck[14] was its architect. Following his swift defeat of the Prussian armies (1871), his "blood and iron" state craft forged a new base for the notions of racial superiority that infested German culture. As anti-Semitism rang through the corridors of schools and universities, it also resounded in the great cathedrals and churches. In 1882 the first international Anti-Semitic Congress[15] was held in Dresden. The press was flooded with anti-Semitic works by Eugen Duhring[16] (progenitor of Nazi ideology) and Heinrich Treitschke.[17] Above all, the works of Houston Stewart Chamberlain[18] poisoned the very air of Germany. Everywhere the intellectual life of the nation was preoccupied with the rot of bigotry.

Chamberlain, an Englishman by birth, betrayed his

native land to join in the emergence of the supernation. According to his "scientific" analysis, history had shown that only the German people were to be considered gifted. As for the prophets and kings of Israel, they too were Aryan, for Chamberlain "showed" the Amorites to be of Teutonic origin. When, on their entrance into Canaan, the Jews conquered them, the Amoritic blood line in the Hebrew population made possible the great men in Israel's history. But what of Jesus, and Paul, and the apostles? That was a simple matter: Palestine was under Roman rule, so many of the soldiers were German by birth. Thus the parentage of Christ and the apostles was proved to be Germanic. Such was the blasphemy being lauded in the churches, such was the nonsense taught in the academies.

From all sides the walls were crumbling. The Catholic bishops blamed the Jews for Bismarck's anticlerical Kulturkampf[19] (1872 to 1879). His Holiness Pius IX[20] took personal charge of Rome's anti-Semitic endeavors on the German front, issuing two encyclicals hostile to the principle of toleration of Jews. Bismarck, meanwhile, reorganized his political base to embrace the support of all the Jew-haters that were crawling out of the gutters and into the Reichstag. It is interesting to read of the ultimate end met by these "statesmen" of prewar Germany. Those who did not quite qualify for the insane asylum found themselves in prison; in some cases, both asylum and prison were to mark their fate. The situation became so debased that in 1891 hundreds of prominent German citizens organized the Society to Combat Anti-Semitism,[21] not out of any love for the Jew, but out of national embarrassment at the depths to which the movement had sunk. Charges of blood libel had sent Germany into a tailspin of turmoil unbefitting a "godlike" people. Wilhelm Marr,[22] one of the "respectables" among the rabble and a leading philosopher of anti-Semitism, forsook his high task with "loathing amounting to nausea."[23] Apparently he did not want to see people practice what he preached.

Vienna became a satellite of Berlin in terms of leading the Austrian states down the primrose path to Hitler. Throughout the Empire the German venom spread and festered out of control. The emperor himself had no stomach for such sordid affairs, as witnessed by his refusal to confirm the election of Dr. Karl Lueger[24] as mayor of Vienna until it appeared that continued refusal might endanger his own position. The good citizens of Vienna threw Lueger at the emperor four times before he was confirmed in his office. His only political dogma was hatred of the Jews, and with this creed he won the support of the good Christians of the Empire.[25]

Westward the tide swept. France became embroiled in the false charge of treason levied against Alfred Dreyfus, a Jewish captain of the artillery accused of spying for Germany. The groundwork for this farce of French history was laid in 1855 with the publication of Count Joseph Arthur Gobineau's four-volume work entitled *Essay on the Inequalities of Human Races.* While Gobineau's influence was restricted, Chamberlain ˚succeeded in re-airing the count's thesis of Aryan superiority and Aryan parentage of the apostles and Christ. It was, however, Edouard Drumont's[26] work *La France Juive* (Judaized France) that set the stage for the entry of France into the column of anti-Semitic nations. In an atmosphere of partisan hatred Drumont began publishing the anti-Semitic paper *La Libre Parole,* in which he again laid the blame for the political turmoil in the country on the Jew. The Third Republic responded by seizing the occasion to drag Dreyfus into the arena for public disgrace and, it was hoped, for appeasement. The hue and cry of "Death to the

Jews" racked the streets of France's great cities until the Third Republic was brought to its knees, with France in disgrace. Dreyfus was ultimately acquitted, promoted, and awarded the "Legion of Honor." The great French novelist Emile Zola had come to the captain's defense in his open letter to Felix Faure (President of France), a letter which won him arrest and self-imposed exile in England. Zola died in London before Dreyfus' vindication, for which he had so vigorously campaigned. In the end, the source of the havoc—the enormous degree of influence wielded by the Jesuits and Dominicans in the Army and Assembly—was exposed and abolished. In 1901 a bloc of anticlerics driven together by the Dreyfus affair succeeded in breaking the power of the church over the education of French youth; and, going further, it severed the connection of church and state which had existed in France since the Concordat between Napoleon I and the papacy. This move dealt French anti-Semitism its death blow.[27]

England's only public response to the German "plague" was the imposition of the Aliens Immigration Act,[28] aimed at stemming the stream of immigrants seeking refuge in her cities. The anti-Semitic implications of the move became public in the debate surrounding its enactment and were subsequently proven false. The Jews did not, in fact, threaten Britain's labor force as contended. Nevertheless, the epidemic had reached the rocky coasts of the sceptered isle. Fortunately it had been caught and diagnosed before the fever spread.

The groundwork had been laid for the unthinkable event that was soon to overtake the Jewry of Europe. As Germany prepared to meet her destiny as master of nations, the world watched and waited. American Jewry rose to the position of benefactor to the world; and as incidents of persecution erupted, American Jews threw their considerable weight into the battle for justice. The first wave of Jewish immigrants began arriving in Palestine or Erez Israel, heralding the rebirth of a national identity. But before that dream was to materialize, the Diaspora community was to pass through the most hideous hour of its history. To the Jewry of the Old World the "Christian" nations held out not justice or truth, but blood and fire.

CHAPTER 14

The Holocaust

Worll War I had exacted a terrible toll from the European nations in terms of both economic ruin and personal tragedy. Germany, the central power to the hostilities, was left floundering in a sea of humiliation, resentment, and deprivation. For twenty years of peace the German people sought an explanation for their ruin, looking everywhere except to the real cause: themselves. Clinging desperately to the myths of Teutonic superiority, Germany stood among her conquerors as a vanquished nation, unwilling to accept the consequences of her humiliation.

It was as though the painful road of civilization had vanished into the underbrush, blocked on every side by internal division, economic distress, and moral degradation. The victorious nations fared no better, for although they could rejoice in their victory, the cost of that glory had been great indeed. Amid the cynicism and grief that are the pallbearers of war, some spoke of a new, hopeful path for mankind based on mutual understanding and the highest resolve for peace. But to a continent in ruin, such hopes were too remote.

Into the vacuum of German life came a group of leaders whose ideological base encompassed all that men have suffered and died to suppress. A new order was to appear in the affairs of men, one based not on the ethical blocks on which civilization stands, but rather on the organized manipulation of all that corrupts the human spirit. National Socialism was the name taken by the messiahs of that new age. The world was to know them simply as Nazis.

From the outset the forgers of the new Germany made no secret of their will to subdue the world and shape it to their own purposes. The lips of the Fuhrer spewed forth the call of the jungle, "I want to see again in the eyes of youth the gleam of the beast of prey. A youth will grow up before which the world will shrink."[1] The world shrank indeed, in disbelief and bewilderment, for human experience afforded no precedent by which mankind could envision the eventualities of such a course. To the demons and gods of darkness the Nazis dedicated their efforts. Never in the remembrance of man had evil stood so boldly exposed. In frenzied lust Germany prepared to meet her destiny. The cause of her ills had been found: the Jews, for it was they who had brought the proudest and noblest of peoples to their knees. Upon their removal, Germany would rise as a phoenix from the flames of her conquest to be master of the earth.

Germany's attempt at self-government—the ill-fated Weimar Republic—floundered in her psychological aversion to such freedom. Order, authority, inevitability— these were concepts Germany understood; and unfortunately for the world, Adolf Hitler also understood them. The terms of the Versailles Treaty, which ended World War I, were renounced (as was the Republic itself) as Jewish treachery. Through terror, assassination, defamation, fraud, and deceit the legions of Nazism wooed the German people.[2] The exploits of the Nazis were common knowledge. Whatever doubts remained were (or should have been) removed with the publication of the new canon *Mein Kampf* (1925). The world of learned men rejected it as a serious threat. The German people read the ravings of their Fuhrer, publicly exalting him with an adulation and obedience born of understanding and approval. Out of a population of sixty-five million, fourteen million Germans stood in the Nazi camp when Hitler seized power in Germany.[3] Central to the Nazi program was the purification of the "human" race. While plans for the destruction or enslavement of nations were kept a secret, the Nazi hierarchy made no attempt to hide its intentions to annihilate the Jews.

The Jew was presented as a parasitic, subhuman phenomenon of decay. Early Nazi policy spoke of "elimination" of the Jews through legal means. Citizenship was revoked, and Jews were methodically removed from public office, the professions, the arts, and the schools. Businesses and private properties were "registered," seized, or destroyed, leading to full-scale impoverization of the Jews.[4] By decree (August 17, 1938) Jews were ordered to adopt as prenames either "Sara" or "Israel."[5] In September, Jewish lawyers were disbarred.[6] In October, 1938, the letter *J* was stamped on all Jewish passports; and by January 1, 1939, mandatory registration cards were being issued.[7] This first phase of the Nazi program was designed to uproot and destroy all cultural bonds between the Jews and Germany and to isolate and degrade Jews so that the "final solution" would find them demoralized and helpless.

Into all the lands of Nazi occupation and influence the nightmare spread. Communities disappeared overnight as Nazi policy rolled on. On September 1, 1939,[8] when Hitler marched into Poland, the second phase of the elimination began. While other peoples also faced a day of reckoning with Hitler (i.e. Poles, Russians, gypsies, non-Russian Communists, etc.), the Jews were his priority. Nazi policy encompassed all Jews—men, women, and children—and all traces of them were to be obliterated. In short, history was to forget they ever existed. In Himmler, Heydrich, and Eichmann the Nazi party had three able practitioners of the exterminator's arts. Their program[9] called for deportations and "concentration" of the Jewish population. Thirty-eight districts were created, from which Jews were herded into cattle cars for "resettlement" in the camps and prisons of the Reich. While preparations for the "final solution" moved on with escalating frenzy, the world remained silent.

As yet, the death machine was not operating at full speed; the Nazis were merely oiling its gears. But it was open season on Jews, who were hunted and beaten to death in the streets, thrown from moving trains, or dragged from hospitals to be buried alive. In schools not yet completely free of Jewish children, "good" little Nazi children were given their Jewish classmates to torture during recess.

Of the approximately twenty million Jews living at the outbreak of the War, about 60 percent of them lived in lands that fell to Hitler. Of these, at least three out of five were to vanish.[10] Auschwitz, Birkenau, Treblinka, Maidanek, Sobibor, Dachau, Muthausen, Buchenwald, Belsen—names that blot the pages of history, names that will haunt man's memory as long as he walks on this earth. From the first year of the war, the purpose of these places was clearly understood. The world was silent; it did not want to believe.

By December of 1942 the truth had become inescapable: Nazi Germany was "exterminating" European

Jewry—outcries, rage, horror, protests, marches, words, words, and more words erupted. The skies of Germany and Eastern Europe grew dark with the smoke of burning flesh. Sophisticated Germans bathed in soap made from human carnage. Lampshades of skin illuminated Nazi parlors, bearing testimony to the success of Hitler's "enlightened" path. Men of science and the arts, scholars and leaders of commerce, met their deaths as torches in the courtyards of German camps. Civilians in towns and villages shot like sheep tens of thousands of their neighbors and former friends. Poison, torture, hanging, burning, freezing, starvation, "experiments"—no method of death was overlooked, no cruelty omitted. The church remained silent. The pope refused to act.[11] Governments failed to act. True, a few raised their voices in tormented protest, and some even mobilized efforts to rescue the doomed;[12] but their numbers were small, their efforts pitifully inadequate. Millions of Christians the world over remained complacent, albeit frustrated. Millions who did act to block Hitler's path met their deaths with the Jewry of Europe.[13] In all, however, the reaction of the Christian world was vague and belated, and it accomplished very little.

The world refused asylum to those who escaped.[14] In the early years of the war, many were turned back into German territories to meet certain death. Immigration laws prevented other nations, including the United States, from absorbing the outcasts. At a time (prior to 1940) when something could have been done to save thousands, nothing was done. Then when it was too late, the world rendered noble lip service to its outrage.

International Jewish organizations poured money and manpower into rescue efforts which saved hundreds; and when it became clear that death was inevitable, the victims themselves rose in defiance.[15] Individual church bishops issued thousands of false baptismal records, but no organized ecclesiastical policy was formed on this matter.[16] Assistance was, therefore, sparse and inconclusive. The Vatican feared the alienation of its Germanic bishops and constituents, and so kept its silence, referring only obliquely to its desire for a more humane conduct of the hostilities.

The Allies took the position that an all-out effort to save the Jews would play into the hands of Hitler's propagandists, who wished to label the war a Jewish War. Their efforts were further restricted by the infamous "White Paper"[17] issued by the British Parliament prior to the outbreak of the war. A strongly pro-Jewish stand was seen as a threat to Allied integrity. Britain itself was committed to the exclusion of Jewish immigrants from Palestine and the strict regulation of those already there. Thus, when in 1943 the Allies met in Bermuda to formulate a plan to ransom Europe's Jews, no action was taken.[18]

In the end, the Jewry of Europe no longer existed. The oft-repeated statistic of six million victims is only another euphemism with which the world sought to ease its conscience. From the Allied term "events of the East" to the pulpit protests of Europe's churchmen, euphemism was universally employed to mask the unthinkable slaughter of innocent human beings. The aftermath of the war found victorious armies of the Allied Powers walking through a world that defied description. In the vaults of German banks lay gold smelted from human teeth; in her hotels, mattresses stuffed with human hair; in her shops, gloves fashioned from human skin. Mortar pink with the tint of human blood, trains laden with the dead and the dying, corpses piled like lumber in the camps, vast graves of a once great and proud people overrun with rats—all of Germany was a vast slaughterhouse. As a whole, the

Holocaust is an event that will forever escape explanation. Responsibility for it rests on every man equally, and, in the end, on no one, for were "justice" to be done, the result would be equally abhorrent.

Flowers and grass now grow in a soil made sacred by the ashes of a people who, so the Nazis hoped, were to disappear forever from human memory. Countless millions of others died in the conflagration, but with a difference: those who perished in the hideous battles of the war died defending that which the world holds to be rational and just. To the survivors of the "final solution" no answer exists to the question, "Why?"

Even after the war's end, the death continued. In the streets of Polish and German towns and villages, the stunned survivors found no peace. Death stalked them even in their flight. To the allied camps in Italy the broken remnants fled. No wish to return to their homes filled their minds, only the horror-stricken urge to run, to escape and forget.[19] Palestine was the goal of many, but those who thought to find sanctuary on the soil of their ancestors were soon to face yet another trial by fire.

The great light of European Jewry had gone out for a time, but the monumental achievements of that "vanished world" will never be forgotten. Literature, science, medicine, education, philosophy, and economics are but a few of the fields in which the Jewry of yesterday benefited all mankind.[20] The victims of the gas chambers and crematoriums have left us a legacy rich in scope and quality. They have also left a nightmare of unequaled proportions to remind us of the base cruelty to which men can give credence.

Along with adults the Nazi conspirators mercilessly destroyed even children. They killed them with their parents in groups and alone. They killed them in children's homes and hospitals, burying the living in the graves, throwing them into flames, stabbing them with bayonets, poisoning, conducting experiments upon them, extracting their blood for the use of the German Army, throwing them into prison and Gestapo torture chambers and concentration camps, where the children died from hunger, torture, and epidemic diseases.[21]

CHAPTER 15

Postwar Jewry

At the end of World War II there was but one desire burning within the Jews of Europe who had survived Hitler: a land of their own. The Zionist movement had for years negotiated with the British government for the right of Jewish refugees to enter Palestine, then under British rule. Although the Labor government made repeated promises to grant this petition, it continued to enforce the White Paper policy despite the wishes of the League of Nations and, later, the United Nations.[1] Britain wooed the Arab World and blockaded the land to which the remnant of Europe's Jews sought to flee. The problems Britain faced for pursuing this course are fairly well-known and, in large measure, invited.

Palestine had been colonized by Jewish immigrants well before the outbreak of the war. Known as the *Yishuv*,[2] this community inaugurated reclamation projects, agricultural settlement (the kibbutzim), industry, and an administrative system that was the forerunner of the Jewish state. Funds for these pioneer ventures came largely from the United States and Britain (through the Jewish National Fund), where the Jewish communities enjoyed an economic status envied by their fellow countrymen.

Elements of the Yishuv, the Haganah[3] being predominant, formed militia units for the protection of Jewish settlements in Palestine. During the postwar period, these units were actively harassed by the British; and, as a result, their efforts during the 1948 war were severely hampered. On July 22, 1946, a radical underground group known as the *Irgun*[4] carried out a program of terrorism against hostile British authorities, climaxed by the bombing of British Army Headquarters and the Secretariat of the Palestine Government (the King David Hotel). On May 4, 1947, the Irgun struck again, this time freeing 200 prisoners from the prison at Acre.

The British responded with attacks on Yishuv settlements and with mass arrests. In 1929 and 1936 these settlements had been the target of Arab mercenary commandos, but this time the attackers were British. Terrorism by the Irgun was denounced by the Yishuv, the Haganah, the Zionist Congress, and world Jewry as a whole; and yet without it, Britain might never have been brought to the realization that its policies were impractical as well as unjust.

By May of 1947 Britain had recognized that its policies were a failure and called on the United Nations to consider a solution to the problem of Palestine.[5] After three weeks of deliberation in the General Assembly, the U.N. appointed a committee of inquiry to submit proposals for the council's consideration. Soviet opposition to Zionist demands had raised grave doubts as to the success of any proposal for partition, but in a surprising move the Soviet bloc announced its support for either a binational Palestinian state or a partition creating a separate Jewish state in part of the land. After Andrei Gromyko[6] made the announcement on behalf of the Soviet government, hopes ran high as the United Nations Special Committee on Palestine began its work.

While the committee met, the world's conscience was pricked once more as the "Exodus 1947"[7] began its ill-fated voyage to Palestine. Carrying 4,500 displaced Jews, the "Exodus" was seized on the high seas by British gunboats and forced to return to its port of embarkation in the South of France. Britain wished to force the disembarkation of the passengers, but the French government would not allow them to do so. For over a month the refugees remained on prison ships off the coast of France while the diplomatic duel over their destiny raged. The refugees stood firm, and in September of the same year Britain transported the beleaguered Jews to the British zone in Germany and forcibly confined them in detention camps. World reaction was decidedly hostile.

On September 16, 1947, the United Nations General Assembly opened its sessions. In its report, the Special Committee called for the partition of Palestine, with Jerusalem and its environs to become an international zone. On November 29 the report was adopted by a vote of 33 to 13.[8] Ten weeks later the final vote was to be taken, the one which would create the State of Israel.

The British Mandatory Power in Palestine immediately adopted a policy of noncooperation with the United Nations' decision. The morning after the initial vote was taken, the Yishuv was again the target of Arab attacks. This time the attackers were foreign mercenaries from neighboring Arab lands, allowed by the British to enter Palestine. As the tempo of the conflict escalated, the day of independence neared.[9] On May 14, 1948, David Ben-Gurion read the proclamation establishing the Third Jewish Commonwealth,[10] to be known as the State of Israel. On the following morning the Provisional Government, taking the reins of State, embarked on its first national effort, to survive the Arab onslaught.

The first nation to recognize the reborn Israel was the

United States, and appropriately so, for President Harry S. Truman had led the American people in support of the creation of the Hebrew nation.[11] A public opinion poll taken in November of 1945 revealed that 80.1 percent of the population favored the establishment of Israel, 9.4 percent were undecided, and 10.5 percent were opposed. The presidential campaign of 1944 found both Republicans and Democrats in agreement on the issue. In a joint resolution of Congress passed in December of 1945 the United States government urged the opening of Palestine to Jewish immigration, so that the work of building toward statehood could begin.[12]

With the establishment and recognition of the State of Israel a fact of history, the Jewry of America found itself in a crucial position. Money was needed to combat the Arab armies and to get the new nation on its feet. The American community joined its counterparts in Europe in raising hundreds of millions of dollars.

The war of 1948 was not simply a war of independence; it was a struggle for life. Leading the Arab ideological cause was the Mufti[13] of Jerusalem, a former Nazi collaborator who had allegedly been actively engaged in the "final solution" of the Nazi Era. True to his calling, he charged the Arab world with completing Hitler's work by annihilating the Jews of Israel on the pretense of waging a "Holy War." The Mufti had fled France and established himself and his lieutenants in Cairo following the war. Ostensibly, the British denied any wrongdoing; yet the fact remains that the Arab League to which the Mufti fled was a British creation.

After more than twenty years, the conflict still rages. But what of the rest of Jewry? Because of the mass emigrations and murders which were the legacy of World War II,

Jewish domicile in the classical centers of anti-Semitism has been greatly reduced. In our decade, the United States, the Soviet Union, and Israel represent the only remaining major centers of Jewish life. A fortunate result of the Nazi era, if indeed there is one, is an international abhorrence of anti-Semitism. This phenomenon can be traced in part to the atmosphere of contrition which pervaded the West following the war. Through ecumenical endeavors, Christendom has sought to remove the centuries-old stigmas concerning the Jew. Although such efforts are laudable, it is also a fact that the church no longer occupies the position of social prominence it did a century ago. These efforts, therefore, do not represent a movement of the magnitude which could be desired.

In the most recent outbreaks of Middle East hostilities, a number of churches have shown evidences of sympathy for Arab-based anti-Zionism, which must admit to being but a hair away from true anti-Semitism.[14] Following the 1967 war, President de Gaulle of France, angered by the massive support given to Israel by French Jewry, characterized the Jews as being an "elitist, self-confident, and domineering people."[15]

Anti-Semitism has followed the flux of history into an era concerned with power and wealth. The Jewish community has enjoyed a share in this new prosperity and a share of the power as well. Hand in hand with these signs of social prominence has come renewed antagonism.

In the racial upheavals of the 1960s,[16] the Jews found themselves a target on both sides. To the Negroes, they represented landlords and businessmen who "got rich" in the ghetto. Jewish support of civil rights activities led to the fear among black organizers that their movement was being taken out of their hands. On the other hand, the white Gentile community was quick to condemn Jewish "exploitation" of blacks, and the more bigoted saw conspiracy in the fight for civil rights. In general, American Jewry has been the last occupant of the ghettos now populated by black Americans.

The present posture of anti-Semitism in the Western bloc is such that it does not pose an immediate threat to those of a Jewish heritage. In the light of modern cultural secularism, the Jewish population is almost invisible. Perhaps this desire to be left alone to live in peace among friends is, again, the result of Gentile hostilities of the past. Some among the Jewish community have no concern for their Jewish identity; others seek to nurture it. In the end, both have the same goal: survival. In this desire to survive we all share; it is forever universal.

It has been said that the Israeli Jew is arrogant and self-serving, totally unconcerned with what the world thinks of him. To an extent, the observation is correct. In the aftermath of two millennia of persecution, an aggressively defensive posture has emerged. It is nonsense to suggest that another nation or people would react differently. The lessons of history have shown that the road of assimilation and compromising of the Jewish identity does not work. That road led to the concentration camp. To condemn modern Jewry for demanding those elements of a secure identity which all people demand (such as a homeland) is indeed hypocritical. Likewise, to condemn Israel as aggressive is strategically implausible.

The net result of the reestablishment of a Hebrew State has been the appearance of a Jewish identity that commands respect and at the same time evokes resentment. The difficult problems posed by Israel's existence have no easy answers either politically or ethically. Aggravating the situation is the thirst of our machines for oil. Once again the Jew stands in the middle.

CHAPTER 16

The Arab World

Relations between Jews and Arabs have always been difficult at best. By the time of the monarchy (The First Commonwealth), the Hebrew tribes had settled into an agrarian social order which stood in sharp contrast to the life of the nomadic tribes in the vast desert areas. Thus, even at that remote point in history the primordial conflict between the farmer and the hunter existed with the sedentary Hebrews and their nomadic Arab kinsmen. That that conflict is timeless is a fact of history.

Social unrest hand in hand with theological struggles and basic human distrust have joined in promulgating the rift between the sons of Israel and the tribes of whom Ishmael is father. Through centuries of interaction Jews and Arabs have known periods of both close cooperation and open hostility. It is impossible for anyone to characterize the common history of the Semitic peoples as either peaceful or warlike. It has been both.

In Spain as well as in Turkey, Jews and Moslems lived in great harmony, as we have seen. Caliphs exerted their considerable influence in attempting to aid their Jewish half brothers suffering persecution in Christian lands. In return, the Jews in Moslem lands brought wealth and brilliance to the royal court. At the opposite end of the

117

story are the periods of pogrom and repression. On the whole, however, relations between Islamic peoples and the Jews were peaceful and productive for centuries. As we move into the area of modern history, however, we find that harmony rapidly disappearing.

The single factor in this move toward hostility has been the Zionist movement, which led to the creation of the State of Israel. From its earliest appearance, the Zionist cause met unremitting opposition from the Arab nations, as well as from many others. As vanguard of the nation to come, the Yishuv in Palestine was the first Jewish body to learn the full degree of that opposition. By a cruel turn of events the establishment of a Jewish homeland followed close on the heels of World War II. The Arab World, which during the war had wavered between pro-Axis and pro-Allied loyalties, was quick to pick up on the anti-Jewish sentiment that had so recently embroiled the European nations. With slight rhetorical modifications, the anti-Semitism of Nazi Germany became the anti-Zionist propaganda of the Arab cause. To this day the Arab nations insist that they are not anti-Semitic, only anti-Zionist. Since Arabs are Semites, they argue, it is inconceivable that they could be anti-Semitic. While the logical validity of this argument is apparent, it is equally apparent that it amounts to semantic hairsplitting.

A few illustrations of official Arab activities should serve to uphold this position. Although anti-Semitic literature has been circulated for centuries in the Christian world, until the late nineteenth century it was, for the most part, unknown in Moslem lands. Following the international furor created by the Damascus Affair,[1] however, this literature began to make its appearance in Arabic.[2] Largely French in origin, these works of hate rapidly caught the attention of the literate and filtered throughout the social structure. In 1869 the *Destruction of the Jewish Religion* was published in Beirut. In 1890 the book was reprinted in the U.A.R. official book series under the title *Talmudic Human Sacrifices. The Talmud Jew*, by August Rohling, was published in Cairo in 1899. The *Protocols of the Elders of Zion* reappeared in a new version as late as 1969, published by the brother of Egypt's President Nasser.[3]

Arab anti-Semitism has, to be sure, been fanned by the Arab-Israeli conflict. It cannot, however, be cited as a cause for this conflict. It is instead an illegitimate child born of war and hatred, used to perpetuate the image of Israel as a colonialist, aggressive regime bent on the subjugation and repression of the Arab World. The propagandists' desire to support their official position led to the interest in and publication of anti-Semitic works which sought to "substantiate" the inherent "evil" of the Jewish State by divulging its origins in Jewish history. Zionism is presented as "the executive mechanism" of Judaism.[4] Although in a political sense this representation is factual, it serves to betray the parallel animosity felt for Zionists and Jews in general.

Arabic anti-Semitic literature has for the most part originated in government circles either as official publications or in public addresses and the media. It cannot be said, therefore, that this body of works exists only on the fringes of Arab society. On the contrary, it lies close to the heart.[5] The *Protocols of the Elders of Zion* stands out as the work most frequently circulated. It was a favorite source of quotes to the late Egyptian President Nasser. Secondary-school books contain blatant anti-Semitic references, as do the official indoctrination manuals used in the military. As early as 1920 the theme of an international Jewish conspiracy was adopted by Arab leaders as the basis for their anti-Zionist activities. The Nazi exterminations have been given a rationale in Arabic publications; and the Arab press has gone so far as to intimate that Adolf Eichmann, himself a martyr, will have a successor to complete his task of annihilation.[6] Arab propagandists have attempted to join the forces of Islam and the Christian world through publications such as Abdullah-al-Tal's *The Dancer of World Jewry Against Islam and Christianity* and M.A. Aluba's "Palestine and Humanity's Conscience." Thus, as for centuries they served the Christian world, anti-Semitic books have served the Arab world in our own time.

Turning to the international ramifications of Arab anti-Semitism, we note that the Arab press does not limit its publications to the Arabic tongue. Propaganda is published in foreign languages as well and circulated through anti-Semitic groups around the world.[7] It should also be noted that Arab anti-Semitism is more official than practical in character. Outside of Morocco, few Jews are left in Arab lands. The unfortunate Jews remaining in Iraq and Syria suffer blatant, although sporadic, social persecution.[8] The continuing conflict in the Middle East will certainly continue to fan the fires of anti-Semitism around the world, both anti-Jewish and anti-Arab. We must be careful not to fall victim to either. In a situation shot through with deep emotional impact it should be remembered that there is never a totally innocent party to a conflict, be he Jew or Arab. Political alignment and sympathy is one thing; ethnic and racial prejudice, quite another. As war follows war in the perhaps unresolvable conflict for territory, hatred grows deeper and becomes more personal. Hopeful notes, however, may be sounded.

Although on both sides of the battle line extremist hate-mongers abound, as they do throughout the world, humanity and moral conscience do, fortunately, still hold sway. Among both Arabs and Jews the light of reason still burns, for as men, both groups recognize the futility of hate. Whether or not an innate feeling for what is right and peaceable can survive the monumental power struggle being waged is yet another unanswered question.

Since 1967 the avalanche of official anti-Semitism has slowed, due to unfavorable reactions to the Arab cause precipitated by it. Granted, the posture of anti-Zionism remains intact, but it appears that at least some Arab leaders have come to the realization that the world powers will not be parties in sympathy to a cause rooted in Nazi ideology. Likewise, public support for extremist groups is no longer considered appropriate to the emerging image of twentieth-century Arab states. Whether or not this apparent softening of anti-Semitic overtones and extremist desperation signals a change in Arab-Jewish relations has yet to be seen. For the mutual benefit of the principal parties to the conflict as well as for the safety of those nations who have intervened in the volatile situation, let us hope that indeed it does.

Epilogue

We have now reached the end of our inquiry into the forces of anti-Semitism, but in fact we have hardly begun to scratch the surface. In order to span a period of almost two millennia we have dealt largely in generalities. A detailed account would be the work of a lifetime and would fill the pages of hundreds of volumes. It is a grim story, one which does not make pleasant reading.

Certainly the Jew is not the only member of the family of man to be the target of monstrous brutality; one need only recall the methodical displacement and cultural destruction of the American Indian in the nineteenth century. Genocide as an instrument of power is not unknown even in our own country. The history of America's Indian Wars drips with the blood of "savage innocents" slaughtered in the interest of national destiny and progress. An unfortunate legacy of Western civilization gives rise to the cultural effeteness that rationalizes and justifies the eradication of "inferior" cultures which stand in the path of the technological revolution. To meet this issue on the most basic level we are confronted with the Darwinian principle of "natural selection": only the strongest will survive. Such is the law of nature, the law of the jungle. Is it also the law of human society?

Hitler's Germany looms ominously in the history of the world. Savage, brutal, amoral, and crazed with the drive for power, Nazism as a social phenomenon has been analyzed and decried for decades; and yet, are not the forces which in Nazi ideology stand so blatantly exposed smouldering just beneath the conscious drives of all men?

Social order serves as a framework of defined behavior calculated to control and suppress these aggressive, destructive impulses. Harnessed by codes of morality and law, this aggression can be directed toward constructive achievement; but left to seek its own outlet, the results are devastating.

Since the conquest of Jerusalem by the crushing armies of Rome, the Hebrew people have been forced to endure an existence based on the "generosity" of the nations to which they have fled. Their history is filled with peaks of brilliance and abysses of despair. That they have survived at all is a miracle of inestimable importance. Few other peoples can trace their roots so far back into the corridors of time. The Hebrew people live in the consciousness of a divine charter, a chosenness which has made of them instruments in the shaping of history. To a barbaric (and yet highly civilized) world they gave the concept of an omnipotent and a merciful God. From the moment of that revelation the course of the world was changed, for an element had been added to the spiritual life of man which would not have arisen within the philosophical systems of the "pagan" world. To the ethical and moral life of man the door was opened on a new age. No longer were societies bound to the cumbersome and merciless mores of pantheistic religions. Judaism prepared the way for the dawn of Christendom, which carried the Western world into the present age.

The very fact of the Diaspora may be said to be the dawn also of the Christian West, for as the exiles fanned out across the Roman world, they carried with them the spiritual soil in which Christianity was to grow. In a world grown tired and cruel, this vanguard of the church proliferated the teachings of the prophets and sages and offered despairing men hope and honor. Indeed, Judaism became a serious threat to Roman authority as its spiritual teachings began to erode the principles upon which Rome's might rested. When the apostolic message of Christ reached Rome's gates, it fell upon eager ears, for its way had been prepared much the same as John had pointed to the coming of Jesus. Within a century of Paul's missionary journeys, the pagan West was literally crushed by the rise of the church. As we have seen, this turn of history was to have grave consequences for those of Hebrew blood who had given it birth. The pagan world proved more hospitable to the Jew than did the Christian world. Persecution of the Jew on the part of the church coincided with its rise to power; and throughout history it has, for the most part, proved unrelenting.

To be sure, the church was not the only quarter from which oppression came. What we see is an illogical perversion of standards and values which served some underlying need to justify the exclusion of the Jew from the larger Christianized society. The church provided both the vehicle and the rationale to accomplish this "setting apart" of the Jew. Theology, called to the forefront of the battle, lashed out against the "infidel" who, after all, had been the instrument of the crucifixion. The astonishing fact is that these poorly (though elaborately) conceived notions have endured for so many centuries. Time after time they have been conjured up to justify whatever atrocity the populace desired to perpetuate upon the Jews. Thus we see how, aside from its direct actions, the Christian church provided indirect avenues of moral anesthesia for nonclerical moves against the Hebrew people.

In the modern era concerted efforts have been made to eradicate all vestiges of anti-Semitism from the Christian community. This move has been accelerated by twinges of conscience resulting from the memory of the Holocaust. While these efforts are laudable, they have come nineteen centuries too late.

Modern anti-Semitism has taken on a secular nature, and threats to the security of the Jewish community no longer follow a theological bent. As our societies have become more complex, our bigotries have become complex as well. The Jew today is the target of a double standard. What is acceptable from Gentiles is not tolerated from Jews. Indeed, what is considered valiant on the one hand is regarded as despicable on the other, as illustrated by the recent appearance of the P.L.O. delegation of the United Nations. Arafat waved an olive branch and brandished a revolver in a speech which can be regarded as nothing less than an ultimatum. He was acclaimed as a freedom fighter and popular hero. But when the Israeli ambassador rose to address the assembly, there was no audience. His statements of Israel's determination to survive were interpreted in some circles as the pronouncements of an arrogant warmonger. In 1948, when the Arab armies overran the intended international zone of Jerusalem and annexed it, they "fought bravely." But in 1967 when Israeli troops retook the city, they "violated international agreements" and "brutally suppressed the Arab population."

By now it is fairly obvious that no logic supports the continuing assaults endured by the Jewish community. Similar activities in other quarters either go unnoticed or elicit admiration; but when the Jewish community exhibits its historical sense of cohesion and exercises its power and influence, it is accused of all manner of unethical behavior.

No simple explanation can be given for the position of the Jew in world history. Some see in it God's judgment; others, a divine plan. Socioeconomic explanations, philosophical pondering, theological treatises, and political analyses—all have been brought to bear on the problem. In the end we can be certain of two things: the Jew will survive, but the prejudice will continue.

Coping with this prejudice is understandably a major concern to the Jewish communities. Bodies like the Anti-Defamation League devote considerable time and effort to the job of recognizing danger signals and dealing with them. This preoccupation is carried even into the arena of Israeli international relations. Security is a primary concern of the relatively new State of Israel. Some of the efforts may appear overzealous or thinly based, but what we must remember is that such judgments come easily to a Gentile community in a position of cultural dominance. Those who seek to make an issue of this Jewish prerogative to avert yet another catastrophe should ponder what it is that causes their own concern.

Numerous anti-Semitic organizations exist the world over; but fortunately their hateful activities attract very few followers. They do pose a threat, however, in the ghosts of doubt and the aspersions which they cast on Jewish communities. Fanatical ideas have a way of diffusing into apparently rational concerns which usually have no foundation in fact. The emotional reaction to these "public" concerns (however fallacious) furnish those of a radical bent with kindling to be fanned and nurtured. Herein lies the greatest danger to the peace and security of the victims, whoever they may be. A very real danger lurks in the subtle and sophisticated maneuverings of organizations and individuals who for whatever reasons strive to manipulate public opinion away from real issues to focus attention on some imagined threat. In the final analysis, everyone becomes the victim; everyone loses. The instigators disappear into the shadows, gloating over their success, while those who have been used to accomplish the task are left with the guilt and the intended victims suffer the bewilderment and pain.

What lessons, then, are to be learned from all these distasteful vistas of history? The answer to this question was given before the history books were ever written. Had it been heeded in a less superficial manner, the tale might not have been told. It can be summed up in the command: "Do to others as you would have them do to you." And yet for all the centuries that the church of Christ has been a force in the world, this simple maxim has defied application in regard to the Jew. Is it any wonder that the great Hillel phrased it differently: "Do not to others as you would have them not do to you."

The "Christian" world has treated the Jew in a manner that is nothing short of a disgrace. We were charged with provoking the Jew to emulation. Yet the church has herded Jews to the baptismal font on pain of death, imprisonment, disenfranchisement, and torture. Those who came of their own will came more likely than not to escape the subtler forms of persecution that pervade the lives of every minority. The Jew, on the other hand, has made serious efforts to assimilate himself, to disappear into the Gentile world. Even then, the Gentile world would not have him.

Let us take little comfort in the present apparently stable state of interfaith relations. One generation of relative calm cannot hope to mark the end of centuries of chaos. The road to brotherhood must lead first through the difficult process of reconciliation. From an historical point of view, it is the church which is obligated to lead the way, and yet at the present time such is not the case. It is fashionable in American life to be pro-Israeli. Such a political position is a comfortable placebo for a troubled conscience. In reality, however, this stance is often nothing but the sort of attitude that vocalizes, "Some of my best friends. . . ." The only foundation on which a real meeting can take place is understanding. This implies that Christians must understand Jews and accept the Jewishness of the Jews as a fact, not as a trait to be changed as the price of that acceptance. Then and only then can a meaningful dialogue begin.

Such dialogues have, in recent years, been organized by various bodies within the Christian community, both Catholic and Protestant. To these overtures the Jewish community has responded with enthusiasm and relief. The day has dawned when a rabbi can stand behind a church pulpit and expound the great prophetic heritage of his faith on which, after all, all of Christendom is based. Likewise, synagogues have opened their doors to the Christian clergy and have listened seriously to the message of the New Testament writers. The only remarkable aspect of this exchange is that it took so long to come about.

Notes

Material on the subject of anti-Semitism is voluminous, and the references supplied here represent but a small portion of that body of literature. References to particular sources for classical writers have, with the exception of Josephus, been omitted.

Chapter 1

1. Charles Raddock, *Portrait of a People* (The Judaica Press Inc.: New York, 1965), vol. 3, pp. 60–61.

2. G. F. Abbott, *Israel in Europe* (Curzon Press, London and Humanities Press: New York, 1971), pp. 1–17.

3. Martin Noth, *The History of Israel* (Harper and Brothers: New York, 1958), pp. 358–69.

4. Flavius Josephus, *The Complete Works of Flavius Josephus,* trans. W. Whiston (Kregel: Grand Rapids, 1963), *Antiquities,* bk. 12, chap. 5, v. 2. See also: I Macc. 1:16–67; II Macc. 5:11–20; Diodorus, *Bibliotheca* 34:1.

5. E. L. Ehrlich, *A Concise History of Israel,* trans J. Barr (Harper and Row: New York, 1965), p. 107.

6. Josephus, *Antiquities,* bk. 13, chap. 8, v. 3.

7. Josephus, *Against Apion,* bk. 1, vv. 73 and 228. See also V. Tcherikover, *Hellenistic Civilization and the Jews* (Jewish Publication Society of America: Philadelphia, 1961), pp. 361–64.

8. Noth, *History of Israel,* p. 424. See also Rufus Leersi, *Israel: A History of the Jewish People* (The World Publishing Co.: Cleveland and New York, 1966), p. 164.

9. Raddock, *Portrait,* vol. 1, p. 143.

10. Noth, *History of Israel,* p. 406. Josephus, *Antiquities,* bk. 14, chap. 10, v. 1. Raddock, *Portrait,* vol. 1, p. 133.

11. Josephus, *Antiquities*, bk. 19, chap. 5, v. 2. See also S. W. Baron, *A Social and Religious History of the Jews* (Columbia University Press and The Jewish Publication Society of America: New York and Philadelphia, 1973), vol. 1, p. 189.

12. Josephus, *Against Apion*, bk. 1, v. 288.

13. Ibid., vv. 304–20.

14. Ibid.

15. See Philostrates, *Vita Apollonia*, 6:29.

16. See Horace, *Satires*, 1:9, 69; 1:5, 100. Max Radin, *The Jews among the Greeks and Romans* (Jewish Publication Society of America: Philadelphia, 1915), pp. 245–49, 399–402.

17. See Martial, *Epigrammation*, 7:55, 4:4, 7:30, 11:94. Radin, *Jews, Greeks, and Romans*, pp. 302, 325–30.

18. See Cicero, *Pro Flacco*. Radin, *Jews, Greeks, and Romans*, pp. 220–35.

19. See P. Cornelius Tacitus, *Historiae*, 5:1–13.

20. See Decimus Junius Juvenal, *Satires*, 14:96–106, 6:542–47, 3:13–16.

21. Baron, *History of the Jews*, vol. 2, p. 106.

Chapter 2

1. Hosea 6:6.

2. J. B. Agnus, *The Meaning of Jewish History* (Abelard-Schuman: London, Toronto, New York, 1963), vol. 1, p. 131.

3. Martin Noth, *The History of Israel* (Harper and Brothers: New York, 1958), p. 466.

4. J. M. Allegro, *The Chosen People* (Doubleday: New York, 1972), p. 295.

5. Rufus Leersi, *Israel: A History of the Jewish People* (The World Publishing Co.: Cleveland and New York, 1966), p. 189. But see also S. W. Baron, *A Social and Religious History of the Jews* (Columbia University Press and The Jewish Publication Society of America: New York and Philadelphia, 1973), vol. 2, p. 9.

6. Noth, *History of Israel*, p. 447.

7. Leersi, *Israel*, p. 189.

8. Noth, *History of Israel*, p. 447.

9. Leersi, *Israel*, p. 190

10. Baron, *History of the Jews*, vol. 2, pp. 121–30.

11. Noth, *History of Israel*, p. 450.

12. M. I. Dimont, *Jews, God, and History* (Simon and Schuster: New York, 1962), p. 111.

13. Leersi, *Israel*, p. 193. See also Max Radin, *The Jews among the Greeks and Romans* (Jewish Publication Society of America: Philadelphia, 1915), pp. 343–44.

14. Leersi, *Israel*, p. 194.

15. Charles Raddock, *Portrait of a People* (The Judaica Press Inc.: New York, 1965), vol. 1, p. 167. Also Deut. 6:4.

16. Cecil Roth, *History of the Jews* (Schocken Books: New York, 1961), p. 116.

17. A. Brooks and W. Sennigen, *A History of Rome to A.D. 565* (The Macmillan Company: New York, 1965), p. 432.

18. Gregory Ostrogorsky, *History of the Byzantine State* (Rutgers University Press: New Brunswick, 1969), p. 44. See also Dimont, *Jews*, p. 151; J. R. Marcus, *The Jew in the Medieval World* (Atheneum: New York, 1972), p. 4.

19. Ostrogorsky, *Byzantine State*, p. 47.

20. Ibid., pp. 49–50. Dimont, *Jews*, p. 154. Marcus, *Jew in Medieval World*, pp. 8–12.

21. Roth, *History of the Jews*, p. 144.

22. J. R. Marcus, *The Jew in the Medieval World* (Atheneum: New York, 1972), p. 5. Ostrogorsky, *Byzantine State*, p. 56. See also C. Pharr et al., eds. and trans., *The Theodosian Code*, 1952; 16:8, 10, 18, 22, 25, 26, 27, 29.

23. Marcus, *The Jew in the Medieval World*, p. 6. Ostrogorsky, *Byzantine State*, p. 75. Andrew Sharf, *Byzantine Jewry* (Schocken Books: New York, 1971), p. 19. See also R. Scholl and W. Kroll, eds., *Corpus Juris Civilis*, 1954; Novella 37, 45, 146.

24. Sharf, *Byzantine Jewry*, pp. 48–49.

25. Leersi, *Israel*, p. 209.

26. Ostrogorsky, *Byzantine State*, p. 104.

27. Ibid., p. 108.

28. Leersi, *Israel*, p. 209. Baron, *History of the Jews*, vol. 3, p. 23.

Chapter 3

1. W. M. Watt, *What is Islam?* (Frederick A. Praeger: New York and Washington, 1968), p. 94.
2. Cecil Roth, *History of the Jews* (Schocken Books: New York, 1961), p. 149.
3. W. M. Watt, *Muhammad* (Oxford University Press: London, 1961), p. 89. A. Guillaume, *Islam* (Penguin Books: Baltimore, 1956), p. 36.
4. Guillaume, *Islam*, p. 39.
5. N. J. Dawood, trans., *The Koran* (The Whitefriars Press: London, 1959), p. 326.
6. Rufus Leersi, *Israel: A History of the Jewish People* (The World Publishing Co.: Cleveland and New York, 1966), p. 225.
7. M. I. Dimont, *The Indestructible Jews* (The New American Library: New York, 1971), p. 132.
8. Leersi, *Israel*, p. 227.
9. R. F. Dibble, *Mohammed* (The Viking Press: New York, 1926). See also S. W. Baron, *A Social and Religious History of the Jews* (Columbia University Press and The Jewish Publication Society of America: New York and Philadelphia, 1973), vol. 3, pp. 64, 79.
10. Watt, *Muhammad*, p. 205.
11. Sir John Glubb, *The Life and Times of Mohammed* (Stein and Day: New York, 1970), p. 359.
12. Charles Raddock, *Portrait of a People* (The Judaica Press Inc.: New York, 1965), vol. 2, p. 53.
13. Baron, *History of the Jews*, vol. 5, p. 8.

Chapter 4

1. S. W. Baron, *A Social and Religious History of the Jews* (Columbia University Press and The Jewish Publication Society of America: New York and Philadelphia, 1973), vol. 3, pp. 12, 189, 229.
2. Andrew Sharf, *Byzantine Jewry* (Schocken Books: New York, 1971), p. 61.

3. Baron, *History of the Jews*, vol. 3, p. 7.

4. Gregory Ostrogorsky, *History of the Byzantine State* (Rutgers University Press: New Brunswick, 1969), pp. 183–84.

5. Baron, *History of the Jews*, vol. 3, p. 27. See also J. R. Marcus, *The Jew in the Medieval World* (Atheneum: New York, 1972), pp. 111–14, 151–54.

6. Ostrogorsky, *Byzantine State*, pp. 205–6. See also Rufus Leersi, *Israel: A History of the Jewish People* (The World Publishing Co.: Cleveland and New York, 1966), p. 242.

7. Baron, *History of the Jews*, vol. 3, p. 105. For historical background see Idris Bell, *Cults and Creeds in Graeco-Roman Egypt* (Philosophical Library, Inc.: New York, 1953).

8. L. Greenburg, *The Jews in Russia* (Yale University Press: New Haven, 1951), pp. 2–3.

9. Baron, *History of the Jews*, vol. 3, pp. 211, 407.

10. Ibid., p. 34. Marcus, *The Jew in the Medieval World*, pp. 101–2.

11. Charles Raddock, *Portrait of a People* (The Judaica Press Inc.: New York, 1965), vol. 2, pp. 53–54. Baron, *History of the Jews*, vol. 3, p. 188.

12. Ibid., pp. 33–36.

13. Ibid., p. 36. H. Graety, *History of the Jews* (Jewish Publication Society of America: Philadelphia, 1894), vol. 3, pp. 37, 46–47.

14. Ibid., p. 37. Marcus, *The Jew in the Medieval World*, pp. 20–23.

15. Baron, *History of the Jews*, vol. 3, p. 43.

16. Ibid., pp. 43, 45. Graety, *History*, vol. 3, p. 108.

17. Leersi, *Israel*, pp. 245–46. G. F. Abbott, *Israel in Europe* (Curzon Press, London and Humanities Press: New York, 1971), p. 60.

18. Baron, *History of the Jews*, vol. 3, p. 161.

19. Ibid., pp. 155, 183.

20. Ibid., p. 156; vol. 7, p. 147. Leersi, *Israel*, p. 252. Marcus, *The Jew in the Medieval World*, pp. 297–300.

21. Baron, *History of the Jews*, vol. 3, p. 158. Leersi, *Israel*, p. 253.

22. Marcus, *The Jew in the Medieval World*, pp. 306–10, 364–66. Baron, *History of the Jews*, index to vols. 1–8, pp. 57–58.

23. Ibid., pp. 100–101.

24. Baron, *History of the Jews*, vol. 4, p. 253, n. 49.

25. Ibid., p. 37.

26. Baron, *History of the Jews*, vol. 3, p. 124. Leersi, *Israel*, p. 255.

27. Baron, *History of the Jews*, vol. 3, pp. 90–91, 272. Leersi, *Israel*, pp. 258–59.

Chapter 5

1. *Encyclopedia Judaica* (Macmillan: New York, 1971), vol. 3, p. 102. H. Graety, *History of the Jews* (Jewish Publication Society of America: Philadelphia, 1894), vol. 3, pp. 164–68.

2. Rufus Leersi, *Israel: A History of the Jewish People* (The World Publishing Co.: Cleveland and New York, 1966), p. 266.

3. S. W. Baron, *A Social and Religious History of the Jews* (Columbia University Press and The Jewish Publication Society of America: New York and Philadelphia, 1973), vol. 4, p. 43.

4. Ibid., p. 49.

5. Ibid., chap. 21.

6. Ibid., p. 96. J. R. Marcus, *The Jew in the Medieval World* (Atheneum: New York, 1972), pp. 115–20.

7. G. F. Abbott, *Israel in Europe* (Curzon Press: London and Humanities Press: New York, 1971), pp. 105–14. Baron, *History of the Jews*, vol. 5, p. 348, n. 59.

8. Marcus, *Jew in Medieval World*, pp. 137–41.

9. Ibid., p. 143.

10. Abbott, *Israel in Europe*, p. 119.

11. Cecil Roth, *A History of the Jews in England* (Oxford University Press: Clarendon, 1964), pp. 85, 68–90.

12. Graety, *History*, vol. 4, p. 46. Marcus, *The Jew in the Medieval World*, pp. 127–30, 155–58.

13. Graety, *History*, vol. 4, pp. 298–99. For a study of the blood libel in its various manifestations see M. I. Seiden, *The*

Paradox of Hate (Thomas Yoseloff: London and New York, 1967). Also included are translations of anti-Semitic works by Tacitus, Cicero, Tertullian, Augustine, etc.

14. Baron, *History of the Jews*, vol. 11, pp. 122–91.
15. Graety, *History*, vol. 4, p. 299.
16. Abbott, *Israel in Europe*, pp. 95, 108. Marcus, *Jew in Medieval World*, p. 147.
17. Graety, *History*, vol. 4, pp. 222, 224–26.
18. Ibid., p. 224.
19. Ibid., pp. 258–60.
20. Ibid., pp. 296–98.
21. Ibid., pp. 202–17.

Chapter 6

1. Cecil Roth, *History of the Jews* (Schocken Books: New York, 1961), pp. 189–205.
2. R. Sabatini, *Torquemada and the Spanish Inquisition* (Stanley Paul Company: London, 1929), pp. 32–33.
3. Roth, *History of the Jews*, pp. 209–17.
4. Rufus Leersi, *Israel: A History of the Jewish People* (The World Publishing Co.: Cleveland and New York, 1966), pp. 303–6. J. R. Marcus, *The Jew in the Medieval World* (Atheneum: New York, 1972), pp. 244–46, 247–50.
5. Cecil Roth, *A History of the Marranos* (Meridian Books Inc.: New York, 1959), p. 13. Charles Raddock, *Portrait of a People* (The Judaica Press Inc.: New York, 1965), vol. 2, p. 74.
6. H. Kamen, *The Spanish Inquisition* (The New American Library: New York, 1965), p. 14.
7. Sabatini, *Torquemada*, pp. 85–86. Leersi, *Israel*, p. 309.
8. Roth, *History of the Jews*, p. 221.
9. Isa. 1:19–20.
10. Roth, *History of the Jews*, p. 200.
11. Ibid., pp. 220–22.
12. Roth, *Marranos*, pp. 32–38.
13. Ibid.

14. Ibid., pp. 39–46.
15. Sabatini, *Torquemada*, pp. 135–67. Marcus, *Jew in Medieval World*, pp. 173–78.
16. Roth, *Marranos*, pp. 51–52.
17. Kamen, *Spanish Inquisition*, p. 23. Marcus, *Jew in Medieval World*, pp. 51–55.
18. Roth, *Marranos*, pp. 271–73.
19. Roth, *History of the Jews*, pp. 226–27. Kamen, *Spanish Inquisition*, pp. 23–24. See also Rabbi L. J. Levinger, Ph.D., *A History of the Jews in the United States* (Union of American Hebrew Congregations: New York, 1949), pp. 23–38.
20. Leersi, *Israel*, p. 317.
21. Roth, *Marranos*, pp. 54–73. Marcus, *The Jew in the Medieval World*, pp. 56–60.

Chapter 7

1. Cecil Roth, *The Jews in the Renaissance* (Harper and Row: New York, 1959), pp. 3–20.
2. H. Graety, *History of the Jews* (Jewish Publication Society of America: Philadelphia, 1894), vol. 4, p. 339, 352–61, 371.
3. Cecil Roth, *History of the Jews* (Schocken Books: New York, 1961), pp. 239–42. Roth, *Jews in Renaissance*, pp. 137–64. See also S. W. Baron, *A Social and Religious History of the Jews* (Columbia University Press and The Jewish Publication Society of America: New York and Philadelphia, 1973), vol. 13, pp. 161–71.
4. Graety, *History*, vol. 4, pp. 491–511. J. R. Marcus, *The Jew in the Medieval World* (Atheneum: New York, 1972), pp. 251–55.
5. Graety, *History*, vol. 4, p. 400.
6. G. F. Abbott, *Israel in Europe* (Curzon Press, London and Humanities Press: New York, 1971), p. 173.
7. Graety, *History*, vol. 4, p. 401.
8. Ibid.
9. Ibid., pp. 575–77. Marcus, *The Jew in the Medieval World*, pp. 411–17.

10. Graety, *History*, vol. 4, pp. 577, 593–98. Marcus, *Jew in Medieval World*, pp. 320–22.

11. Graety, *History*, vol. 4, pp. 602–3, 627–30.

12. Ibid., pp. 619–26; vol. 5, pp. 51–54, 118–21.

13. Abbott, *Israel in Europe*, p. 233.

14. Ibid., pp. 233–34. Roth, *Jews in Renaissance*, pp. 127–28.

15. Rufus Leersi, *Israel: A History of the Jewish People* (The World Publishing Co.: Cleveland and New York, 1966), pp. 335–37. Marcus, *The Jew in the Medieval World*, pp. 170–72.

16. Marcus, *The Jew in the Medieval World*, pp. 166–67.

17. Ibid., pp. 167–69.

18. See Glock and Stark, *Christian Beliefs and Anti-Semitism* (Harper and Row: London and New York, 1966).

19. Baron, *History of the Jews*, vol. 13, pp. 285–91.

20. See Chapter 10, n. 2.

21. Abbott, *Israel in Europe*, pp. 232–44.

22. Ibid., pp. 196–213.

Chapter 8

1. Cecil Roth, *A History of the Marranos* (Meridian Books Inc.: New York, 1965), pp. 350–51, 354.

2. H. M. Rabinowicz, *The Legacy of Polish Jewry* (Thomas Yoseloff: New York, 1965), pp. 20–24. J. R. Marcus, *The Jew in the Medieval World* (Atheneum: New York, 1972), pp. 205–11.

3. S. Sharp, *Poland, White Eagle on a Red Field* (Harvard University Press: Cambridge, 1953), p. 27.

4. Rufus Leersi, *Israel: A History of the Jewish People* (The World Publishing Co.: Cleveland and New York, 1966), p. 355.

5. O. Halecki, *A History of Poland* (J. M. Dent and Sons Ltd.: London, 1955), pp. 153–56. Marcus, *Jew in Medieval World*, pp. 450–53.

6. Halecki, *History of Poland*, p. 157.

7. Leersi, *Israel*, pp. 359–60.

8. H. Graety, *History of the Jews* (Jewish Publications Society of America: Philadelphia, 1894), vol. 5, pp. 118–55. M. I.

Dimont, *Jews, God, and History* (Simon and Schuster: New York, 1962), pp. 227–28. Marcus, *Jew in Medieval World*, pp. 261–69.
9. Graety, *History*, vol. 5, pp. 152–53.

Chapter 9

1. B. Martin, *A History of Judaism* (Basic Books, Inc.: New York, 1974), vol. 2, pp. 189–92.
2. Ibid., pp. 203–5.
3. See A. Hertzberg, *The French Enlightenment and the Jews* (Columbia University Press: New York, 1968).
4. Martin, *Judaism*, pp. 191–92. For a more extensive study of Enlightenment thinkers see E. Cassirer, *The Philosophy of the Enlightenment* (Beacon Press: Boston, 1955).
5. A. Altman, *Moses Mendelssohn, A Biographical Study* (University of Alabama Press: Alabama, 1973), pp. 569–80.
6. Ibid., pp. 113–16. Rufus Leersi, *Israel: A History of the Jewish People* (The World Publishing Co.: Cleveland and New York, 1966), p. 387.
7. E. Jospe, ed., *Moses Mendelssohn, Selections from His Writings* (The Viking Press: New York, 1975), pp. 183–204. Altman, *Mendelssohn*, pp. 140–58.
8. Jospe, *Mendelssohn Selections*, pp. 15–16. Altman, *Mendelssohn*, pp. 368–73. M. I. Dimont, *Jews, God, and History* (Simon and Schuster: New York, 1962), pp. 298–300.
9. Jospe, *Mendelssohn Selections*, pp. 12–13, 80–81, 87–88. Altman, *Mendelssohn*, pp. 421–552.
10. Jospe, *Mendelssohn Selections*, pp. 10–13. Altman, *Mendelssohn*, p. 729. Charles Raddock, *Portrait of a People* (The Judaica Press Inc.: New York, 1965), vol. 3, pp. 286–87.
11. Jospe, *Mendelssohn Selections*, p. 99.

Chapter 10

1. M. Schappes, ed., *A Documentary History of the Jews in the United States 1654–1875* (The Citadel Press: New York, 1950), pp. 68–69.

2. Rabbi L. J. Levinger, Ph.D., *A History of the Jews in the United States* (Union of American Hebrew Congregations: New York, 1949), pp. 101–12.

3. Ibid., pp. 108–9

4. Lev. 25:10.

5. Levinger, *Jews in U.S.*, pp. 109–10. For an extensive study see D. Runes, *The Hebrew Impact on Western Civilization* (The Citadel Press: New York, 1965), pp. 1–61.

6. Schappes, *Jews in U.S.*, pp. 79–80.

7. Ibid., pp. 80–81.

8. Levinger, *Jews in U.S.*, pp. 133–34. Rufus Leersi, *Israel: A History of the Jewish People* (The World Publishing Co.: Cleveland and New York, 1966), p. 400.

9. Levinger, *Jews in U.S.*, pp. 136–38.

10. Levinger, *Jews in U.S.*, pp. 134–36. For an extensive study see Leon Huhner, *The Struggle for Religious Liberty in North Carolina* (American Jewish Historical Society), vol. 16, p. 37.

11. Levinger, *Jews in U.S.*, p. 134. Leersi, *Israel*, p. 400.

12. G. F. Abbott, *Israel in Europe* (Curzon Press, London and Humanities Press: New York, 1971), p. 297.

13. H. Graety, *History of the Jews* (Jewish Publication Society of America: Philadelphia, 1894), vol. 5, pp. 450–52.

14. Leersi, *Israel*, p. 402.

15. Ibid., p. 404.

16. Graety, *History*, vol. 5, pp. 517–18.

17. Ibid., pp. 458–59, 463–65.

18. Ibid., pp. 476–500.

19. Ibid., pp. 499–502.

20. Ibid., pp. 513–20.

21. Ibid., pp. 528–35.

22. J. Parkes, *A History of the Jewish People* (Quadrangle Books: Chicago, 1962), pp. 195–96. See also B. W. Segel, *The Protocols of the Elders of Zion—the Greatest Lie in History* (Bloch Publishing Co.: New York, 1934). N. Cohn, *Warrant for Genocide* (Harper and Row: New York and Evanston, 1967).

Chapter 11

1. P. G. J. Pulzer, *The Rise of Political Anti-Semitism in Germany and Austria* (John Wiley and Sons, Inc.: New York, 1964), p. 276.
2. Werner Sombart, *The Jews and Modern Capitalism* (T. Fischer Unwin: London, 1913).
3. Pulzer, *Political Anti-Semitism*, pp. 249–50. K. A. Schleunes, *The Twisted Road to Auschwitz* (University of Illinois Press: Urbana and Chicago, 1970) pp. 21–23.
4. Schleunes, *Auschwitz*, pp. 15–24.
5. Ibid., pp. 26–28. Pulzer, *Political Anti-Semitism*, pp. 236–37.
6. Schleunes, *Auschwitz*, pp. 26–33. Pulzer, *Political Anti-Semitism*, pp. 49–52.
7. Pulzer, *Political Anti-Semitism*, pp. 88–101.

Chapter 12

1. L. Greenberg, *The Jews in Russia* (Yale University Press: New Haven and London, 1944–1951), vol. 1, p. 8.
2. Ibid., p. 5.
3. Ibid., pp. 7–8. M. Dubnow, *A History of the Jews in Russia and Poland*, trans. Friedlander (Jewish Publication Society of America: Philadelphia, 1916–1920), vol. 1, pp. 242–61.
4. Greenberg, *Jews in Russia*, vol. 1, pp. 9, 11.
5. Ibid., p. 42.
6. Ibid., pp. 10, 29, 41.
7. Ibid., p. 45.
8. Ibid., p. 31. Rufus Leersi, *Israel: A History of the Jewish People* (The World Publishing Co.: Cleveland and New York, 1966), p. 454.
9. Leersi, *Israel*, p. 455.
10. Ibid., I. Levitats, *The Jewish Community in Russia: 1772–1844* (Columbia University Press: New York, 1943), pp. 35–45.

11. Greenberg, *Jews in Russia*, vol. 1, p. 48.

12. Ibid., p. 45.

13. Ibid., p. 33.

14. Ibid., p. 39.

15. Leersi, *Israel*, p. 463.

16. Greenberg, *Jews in Russia*, vol. 1, pp. 11, 73–75.

17. Ibid., p. 79.

18. Ibid., pp. 81, 104, 119.

19. Ibid., pp. 123, 148, 150.

20. Ibid., p. 92.

21. Ibid., pp. 93, 98.

22. Ibid., p. 158, n. 62.

23. Greenberg, *Jews in Russia*, vol. 2, pp. 19, 24.

24. Leersi, *Israel*, p. 475.

25. Greenberg, *Jews in Russia*, vol. 2, p. 30.

26. Ibid., pp. 34, 49, 86.

27. Ibid., p. 38.

28. Ibid., p. 69.

29. Leersi, *Israel*, p. 480.

30. Greenberg, *Jews in Russia*, vol. 2, p. 169.

31. Ibid., pp. 80, 103.

32. Leersi, *Israel*, p. 533.

33. Greenberg, *Jews in Russia*, vol. 2, pp. 88, 98.

34. Ibid., p. 118.

35. Ibid., p. 58.

36. Ibid., p. 153. See also K. Marx, *A World Without Jews*, trans. D. D. Runes (The Philosophical Library Inc.: New York, 1959).

37. Leersi, *Israel*, p. 535.

Chapter 13

1. Rabbi L. J. Levinger, Ph.D., *A History of the Jews in the United States* (Union of American Hebrew Congregations: New York, 1949), p. 200.

2. Ibid., p. 205. For a detailed study see S. Joseph, *Jewish*

144   A HISTORICAL SURVEY OF ANTI-SEMITISM

ref*Immigration to the United States* (Arno Press and The New York Times: New York, 1969).

3. Levinger, *Jews in the U.S.*, pp. 293–96, 496–99. A. Karp, ed., *The Jewish Experience in America* (American Jewish Historical Society and KTAV Publishing House Inc.: Waltham and New York, 1969), vol. 5, pp. 208–48.

4. Levinger, *Jews in the U.S.*, pp. 252–54, 286–87.

5. Ibid., p. 359.

6. O. and M. F. Handlin, *Danger in Discord* (Anti-Defamation League of B'nai B'rith: New York, 1964). See also C. McWilliams, *A Mask for Privilege* (Little Brown and Company: Boston, 1948), pp. 113–83. For an account of Henry Ford's anti-Semitic activities see Levinger, *Jews in the U.S.*, p. 358; Charles Raddock, *Portrait of a People* (The Judaica Press Inc.: New York, 1965), vol. 3, p. 197.

7. Levinger, *Jews in the U.S.*, p. 365.

8. Ibid., p. 369.

9. Ibid., p. 369–71.

10. Rufus Leersi, *Israel: A History of the Jewish People* (The World Publishing Co.: Cleveland and New York, 1966), pp. 443–44. P. G. J. Pulzer, *The Rise of Political Anti-Semitism in Germany and Austria* (John Wiley and Sons Inc.: New York, 1964), pp. 7–8.

11. U. Tal, *Christians and Jews in Germany*, trans. N. J. Jacobs (Cornell University Press: Ithaca and London, 1975), pp. 118–20.

12. Cecil Roth, *A History of the Jews in England* (Oxford University Press: Clarendon, 1964), p. 266.

13. Leersi, *Israel*, p. 443. G. Bolton, *The Roman Century* (The Viking Press: New York, 1971), pp. 49–78.

14. Pulzer, *Political Anti-Semitism*, pp. 97–99. Tal, *Christians and Jews*, pp. 228–29.

15. Tal, *Christians and Jews*, pp. 247–48. Pulzer, *Political Anti-Semitism*, p. 103.

16. Pulzer, *Political Anti-Semitism*, pp. 52–55.

17. Ibid., pp. 249–50. Tal, *Christians and Jews*, pp. 65–68.

18. Tal, *Christians and Jews*, pp. 280–89.

19. Ibid., pp. 81–118, 223–79. Pulzer, *Political Anti-Semitism*, pp. 271–78.

20. Tal, *Christians and Jews*, p. 101.

21. Leersi, *Israel*, p. 506.

22. Pulzer, *Political Anti-Semitism*, pp. 49–52. Tal, *Christians and Jews*, pp. 259–62.

23. Leersi, *Israel*, p. 507.

24. Pulzer, *Political Anti-Semitism*, p. 185.

25. Ibid., pp. 167–69, 205–6, 341–42.

26. M. R. Marrus, *The Politics of Assimilation* (Oxford University Press: Oxford, 1971), pp. 14–15, 125, 141–42, 197, 206.

27. Ibid., pp. 164–242. M. I. Dimont, *Jews, God, and History* (Simon and Schuster: New York, 1962), pp. 324–27. Leersi, *Israel*, pp. 510–13.

28. Roth, *Jews in England*, pp. 268–70.

Chapter 14

1. Rufus Leersi, *Israel: A History of the Jewish People* (The World Publishing Co.: Cleveland and New York, 1966), p. 592.

2. J. Parkes, *A History of the Jewish People* (Quadrangle Books: Chicago, 1962), pp. 205–6. N. Levin, *The Holocaust* (Thomas Y. Crowell Co.: New York, 1968), pp. 20–27.

3. Charles Raddock, *Portrait of a People* (The Judaica Press Inc.: New York, 1965), vol. 3, p. 179.

4. Ibid., pp. 180–82. Parkes, *History of Jews*, pp. 206–9. Levin, *Holocaust*, pp. 68–73. Cecil Roth, *History of the Jews* (Schocken Books: New York, 1961), pp. 381–82. R. Hilberg, ed., *Documents of Destruction* (Quadrangle Books: Chicago, 1971), pp. 16–24.

5. Levin, *Holocaust*, p. 75.

6. Hilberg, *Documents*, pp. 24–25.

7. Levin, *Holocaust*, p. 78.

8. Ibid., p. 149.

9. Parkes, *History of Jews*, pp. 217–22. Hilberg, *Documents*, pp. 85–106. G. Reitlinger, *The Final Solution* (Thomas Yoseloff: South Brunswick and New York, 1968), pp. 24–30.

10. Roth, *History of Jews*, pp. 407–8.
11. Levin, *Holocaust*, pp. 684–93.
12. Ibid., pp. 667–98.
13. M. I. Dimont, *The Indestructible Jews* (The New American Library: New York, 1971), p. 277.
14. Levin, *Holocaust*, pp. 76–77. Reitlinger, *Solution*, pp. 20–24. Parkes, *History of Jews*, pp. 209–12.
15. R. Ainsztein, *Jewish Resistance in Nazi-Occupied Eastern Europe* (Barnes and Noble: New York, 1974), pp. 463–849.
16. Hilberg, *Documents*, pp. 180–83.
17. Roth, *History of Jews*, pp. 405–7.
18. Levin, *Holocaust*, pp. 539–40.
19. Ibid., pp. 699–713. Roth, *History of Jews*, pp. 407–10. A. Eban, *My People* (Behrman House, Inc. and Random House: New York, 1968).
20. See H. M. Rabinowicz, *The Legacy of Polish Jewry 1919–1939* (Thomas Yoseloff: New York, 1965).
21. Robert H. Jackson, chief American prosecutor at Nuremberg war crimes trials; October 1945.

Chapter 15

1. A. Eban, *My People* (Behrman House, Inc. and Random House: New York, 1968), pp. 431–34.
2. M. I. Dimont, *Jews, God, and History* (Simon and Schuster: New York, 1962), p. 395.
3. Rufus Leersi, *Israel: A History of the Jewish People* (The World Publishing Co.: Cleveland and New York, 1966), pp. 665–66.
4. Ibid., p. 667.
5. Eban, *My People*, p. 438. B. Martin, *A History of Judaism* (Basic Books, Inc.: New York, 1974), vol. 2, p. 347.
6. Leersi, *Israel*, p. 670.
7. Ibid., pp. 670–71. Martin, *Judaism*, vol. 2, pp. 439–40.
8. Eban, *My People*, pp. 442–44.
9. Ibid., pp. 444–52. Leersi, *Israel*, pp. 672–73.

10. Eban, *My People,* pp. 453–58.

11. Ibid., p. 258.

12. Leersi, *Israel,* p. 676.

13. Ibid., pp. 663–65. N. Levin, *The Holocaust* (Thomas Y. Crowell Co.: New York, 1968), pp. 135–36. G. Reitlinger, *The Final Solution* (Thomas Yoseloff: South Brunswick and New York, 1968), pp. 27–28.

14. Martin, *Judaism,* vol. 2, pp. 432–33. M. Himmelfarb, *The Jews of Modernity* (Basic Books Inc.: New York, 1973) pp. 352–53. Epstein and Forster, *The New Anti-Semitism* (McGraw-Hill: New York, 1974) pp. 79–90. *Encyclopedia Judaica* (Macmillan: New York, 1971) vol. 3, pp. 137–38.

15. Martin, *Judaism,* vol. 2, pp. 343–44, 388. *Encyclopedia Judaica,* vol. 3, p. 138.

16. Himmelfarb, *Jews of Modernity,* pp. 181–89, 348. Epstein and Forster, *New Anti-Semitism,* pp. 175–220. See also S. Katz, ed., *Negro and Jew; an Encounter in America* (Macmillan and Co.: New York, 1967).

Chapter 16

1. H. Graety, *History of the Jews* (Jewish Publication Society of America: Philadelphia, 1894), vol. 5, pp. 632–66.

2. *Encyclopedia Judaica* (Macmillan: New York, 1971), vol. 3, p. 138.

3. Epstein and Forster, *The New Anti-Semitism* (McGraw-Hill: New York, 1974), p. 159.

4. *Encyclopedia Judaica,* vol. 3, p. 138.

5. Epstein and Forster, *New Anti-Semitism,* p. 162.

6. Ibid., pp. 158–64, 317–18. *Encyclopedia Judaica,* vol. 3, p. 147.

7. Epstein and Forster, *The New Anti-Semitism,* pp. 159, 162, 165–74.

8. Ibid., pp. 156–58.